How they lived in CITIES LONG AGO

R.J. UNSTEAD

Arco Publishing, Inc.

New York

Author
R. J. Unstead

Editor
Adrian Sington

Published 1981 by Arco Publishing, Inc.
219 Park Avenue South, New York, N.Y. 10003

© Grisewood & Dempsey Ltd 1980

ISBN 0-668-05188-4
Library of Congress Catalog Card No. 81-66504

Printed and bound in Hong Kong by South China Printing Co.

Contents

Seven Ancient Cities

In this book, we are going to look at the layout and buildings of seven ancient cities and, as far as we can, examine the everyday lives of the people who lived in them. The end-paper map shows that the cities were situated – indeed, still are situated – in five areas in which the world's first civilizations arose – the Yellow River basin of northern China; the Indus Valley, in Pakistan in the sub-continent of India; Mesopotamia, which is now called Iraq; the Mediterranean region; and Mexico in Central America.

You will notice that all these areas are practically on the same latitude and that they are separated from one another by immense dis-

tances. The civilizations which grew up in them were also separated by great stretches of time. Mesopotamia and Egypt began about five thousand years ago, while the Aztec civilization of Mexico flourished from about AD 1300. Each started with little or no outside help yet all these civilizations were alike in a number of ways.

This picture of a harvest scene in Ancient Egypt illustrates one of the features common to all early civilizations – large-scale food production. Only when peasants could be organized to produce the food that was needed to feed all the nobles, architects, builders, craftsmen, priests and scribes could a civilization arise and flourish.

The cattle have been domesticated and tread out the grain as men fork away the spent ears. In the foreground a donkey carries away two panniers of grain to the harbour for transportation to the city.

Chapter One

Cradles of Civilization

A famous philosopher named Thomas Hobbes thought that our Stone Age ancestors lived in a state of perpetual fear and misery, an existence that was 'poor, nasty, brutish and short'.

In all probability, it was nothing of the sort. As long as there were plenty of animals, hunters could get all the food they wanted for much less hard work than would have been needed to grow crops. Moreover, they could come and go as they pleased, for there was no-one to order them about, except perhaps the headman of the family group.

But this way of life depended on low numbers. Even when vast herds of mammoth, bison, wild horses and giant rodents roamed the earth, there had to be no more than two or three persons per square kilometre preying on them. So the hunters kept the population down, probably through infanticide, that is, by killing off unwanted children, by neglect or abandoning them on the march. Only if some disaster occurred to reduce the herds or if the population suddenly increased, would it be necessary to abandon hunting and find new ways to obtain food. And both these things did happen.

About 11,000 years ago, the weather became warmer. The great glaciers melted and retreated towards the Poles, so that, in the Northern Hemisphere, grassy plains which had supported great herds became covered with forest, causing many of the big animals like the mammoth, woolly rhinoceros and giant elk to die out, while the numbers of wild cattle, horses and deer were sharply reduced. The same thing happened in the Americas, where nearly all the large animals became extinct. In some parts of the world, lower rainfall turned large areas into desert.

In these conditions, the big-game hunters had to turn their attention to smaller creatures such as deer, wild boar, sheep and goats. Fishing and collecting shell-fish, nuts, edible plants and seeds became ever more important.

Farming began in an area where the wild ancestors of sheep and goats, cattle and pigs had their home and where grain-bearing grasses, the early types of wheat and barley, grew naturally – that is, in the Near East, in the watered uplands of Anatolia (Asia Minor or Turkey), Syria and Palestine. The start of settled village life began in this region, where in about 8000 BC, a people called Natufians built what was the world's first town at Jericho; around 6000 BC, Catal Huyuk in Anatolia had a population of perhaps six thousand persons who lived by growing crops and keeping cattle and goats.

Population explosion

Population increased rapidly as soon as people gave up hunting to live a settled life as farmers. One reason was the change of diet, for it seems to be a fact that men and women who live almost entirely on meat produce fewer children than those living mainly on grain foods. Furthermore, whereas small children would be a handicap to a hunting group forever on the move, they could thrive and soon be useful in a farming community, so there would be no need to keep their numbers down by infanticide.

'To be ignorant of what happened before you were born is to be ever a child.'
Marcus Tullius Cicero (106-43 BC).

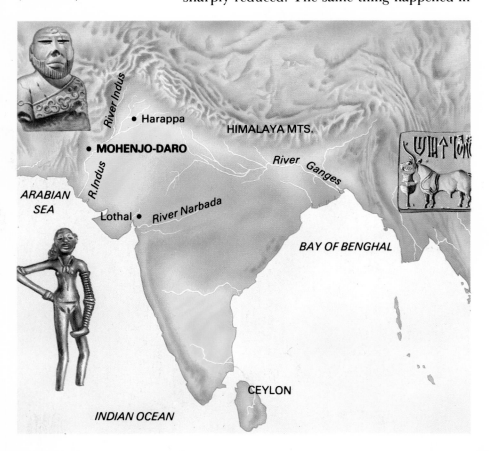

In the valley of the Indus river of Pakistan there arose in about 2500 BC a widespread civilization whose principal cities were Mohenjo-Daro, Harappa and the port of Lothal.
On this map are pictures of three finds from Indus excavations: the limestone bust of a so-called priest-king whose brutal expression has not lost its menace, a delightful bronze figure of a pert little dancing-girl, naked except for her necklace and bangles and one of the stamp seals (possibly used by merchants) with writing on it which we do not understand and an ox-like beast with a single horn.

It was probably increasing numbers that caused some family groups to move away and found new settlements and thereby spread knowledge of farming into neighbouring lands. Yet it was not these communities that produced the first civilizations. They arose in the flat dreary river valleys of Mesopotamia and Egypt and, somewhat later, in India and China.

When peoples with some knowledge of simple farming penetrated these areas, they found that the fertile soil could be made to produce abundant food and, since the soil did not get exhausted, there was no need to move on. They could settle in permanent homes and, as food supplies increased and the population multiplied, their ways of life began to change into completely new patterns.

These changes did not take place suddenly, for it took people a very long time to advance from a state of barbarism. Even after they had taken to farming and living settled lives in villages, hundreds, even thousands of years had to pass before they reached a way of life that might be called civilized.

It was no accident that the world's first great civilizations of Mesopotamia, Egypt, the Indus Valley and the Yellow River arose in river plains of rich alluvial soils that could be made to yield large crops. Even so, they were so isolated that they had no-one to learn from and had to invent things and find out others for themselves, such as how to irrigate the land, to use the wheel for pottery and transport, to store food, to build cities and to keep records in a kind of writing.

The breakthrough generally came when one outstanding man, a genius like Hammurabi, brought a number of separate, perhaps warring, communities under his rule and transformed them into a single kingdom. The first essential was a food surplus, since it enabled some people to do other things than just work on the land. They included the clever ones who became the rulers, craftsmen, architects, artists, merchants, priests and scribes and, gradually, they created an organised society called a state, in which people were divided into classes – nobles, soldiers, officials and so on, down to the peasants whose toil produced the wealth which a civilization needed.

In this book, we have tried not to look at the ancient civilizations as though they were mere stages in a progress towards our own 20th-century civilization; we hope, rather, that you will regard each as a way of life in its own right, whose achievements we can admire and from whose failures we can learn.

This picture map of Egypt shows features which are common to several early civilizations: a great river flowing across an arid land, creating as it moves towards its many-mouthed delta, the narrow strip of fertile watered soil which produces abundant crops. On its banks, or nearby, stand cities (Akhetaten, shown here, is only one of many), colossal temples, statues and the tombs of Kings. Every civilization creates at least two out of the following three features: (1) cities (2) a written language (3) massive ceremonial buildings, such as temples and palaces.

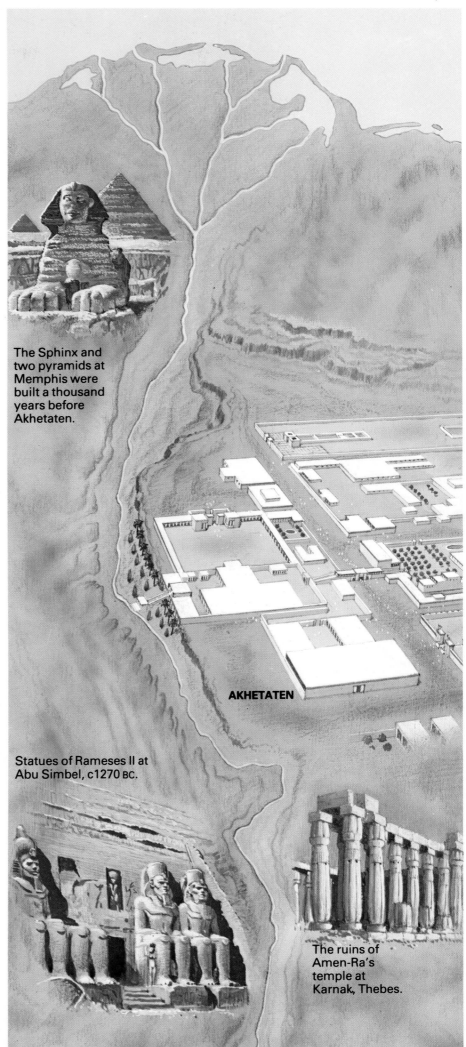

The Sphinx and two pyramids at Memphis were built a thousand years before Akhetaten.

AKHETATEN

Statues of Rameses II at Abu Simbel, c1270 BC.

The ruins of Amen-Ra's temple at Karnak, Thebes.

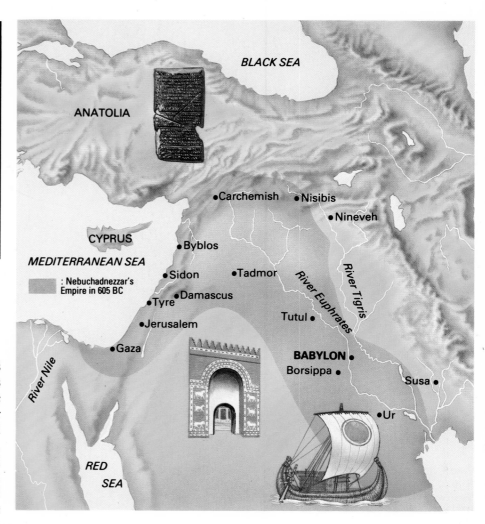

China Becomes Civilized

The popular idea that Chinese civilization is the oldest in the world is not correct, for it dates from about 1750 BC, when the first king of the Shang dynasty began to rule the Yellow River area, having overthrown the last of the so-called Hsia 'emperors', of whom we know very little. At that time, the civilizations of Egypt and Sumer were already over a thousand years old. From the remains of 'Peking Man', discovered near Peking in 1927, we know that Stone Age hunters were living in northern China half a million years ago and that, from about 4000 BC, their descendants were growing crops of wheat and millet and raising pigs, cattle, sheep and dogs. They lived in large fortified villages, made cloth and attractive pottery and had learned how to irrigate their fields and to lessen the effects of the river's annual floods by digging canals.

The soil was very fertile, for it was *loess*, a fine yellowish dust, wind-borne from the deserts of Asia; given moisture, it produced marvellous crops, but the great river valley was subject to floods, tempests, droughts and severe winters, so that the Chinese became accustomed to famine and periodic disaster.

Under the Shangs, many towns were built, trade flourished, bronze weapons and implements came into general use and Shang craftsmen produced jade and bronze vessels of amazing beauty. Astronomers worked out an accurate calendar, horse-drawn chariots were invented and the earliest form of Chinese writing made its appearance on the flat shoulder-blades of cattle. Called Oracle Bones, they bore scratch marks made by priests to obtain magical answers to royal enquiries, such as should the king declare war or build a new town. The emperors governed through a feudal system: the empire was divided into districts governed by loyal rulers who promised to send men to fight for the emperor in return for protection.

In 1027 BC, Shang was overthrown by the Chou, a new dynasty from the west which lasted for nearly eight centuries, during which there was a lot of fighting between war-mongering nobles. Nevertheless, great progress was made. Ox-ploughs and iron tools came into use and a succession of brilliant scholars, among them Confucius, produced books of poetry, hymns and philosophy. The other influential Chinese philosophies were Taoism, conceived by Laotze, and Buddhism. The Chinese also realised the importance of leisure and devised numerous ways to entertain each other. There were bull-fights, cock-fights and board games such as *liu-po*, a game played with six bamboo sticks thrown out of a cup.

With the decline of the Chou, China fell into a period of anarchy. Separate kingdoms made war upon each other, until one of them the Ch'in, defeated the rest and restored order. Its ruler, Huang Ti, was a genius, who created the first Chinese empire, built the Great Wall and a splendid capital at Sian also called Chang-an. But his régime was so harsh that, soon after his death, in 210 BC, the Ch'in were overthrown and replaced by the Han dynasty, founded by a peasant leader named Lin Pang. In AD 25, the capital of China was moved to Loyang. Loyang became the centre of a civilization that was already highly advanced and which was hardly to change until the present century.

It is Han China, with its capital, Loyang, seen on the map opposite, which we shall describe later in this book, a period when China reached one of its many tremendous peaks of splendid achievement.

This map shows 'the Land of Shinar', the great plain watered by the Euphrates and the Tigris as they flowed towards the Persian Gulf. Here was the seat of the world's earliest civilization — Sumer, whose principal city-states were Eridu, Ur, Uruk and Lagash. King Hammurabi won control of the whole country in about 1800 BC and made Babylon its capital. Shown here are three symbols of the Babylonian civilization: a tablet of cuneiform writing, the Ishtar Gate and one of the reed ships that sailed to Egypt and India.

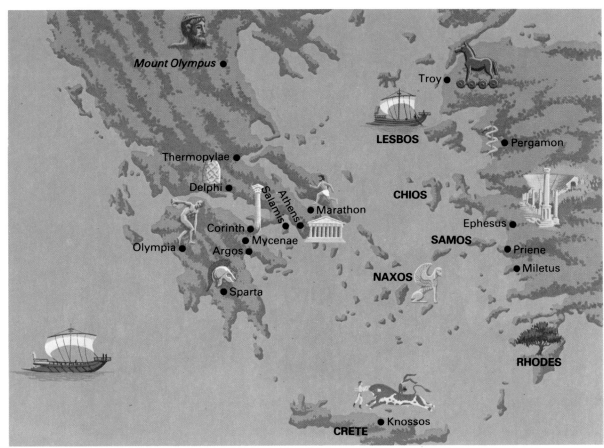

Above: Greece, lying close to Asia and Egypt, came into contact at an early date with ancient civilizations. Minoan Crete flourished between 3000 and 1400 BC, at much the same time as Mycenae on the Greek mainland. Dorian invaders brought disaster but, from the ruins, arose a new Greek or *Hellenic* civilization, centred on the Aegean Sea. Its Golden Age lasted only 30 years (c460-430 BC) but Greek civilization had a lasting influence on the Western world.

Below: This map of modern China shows the boundaries of the ancient Ch'in and Han empires. The symbols are the guardians of the four winds: the snake and tortoise in the north; the red bird in the south; the green dragon in the east; and the white tiger in the west.

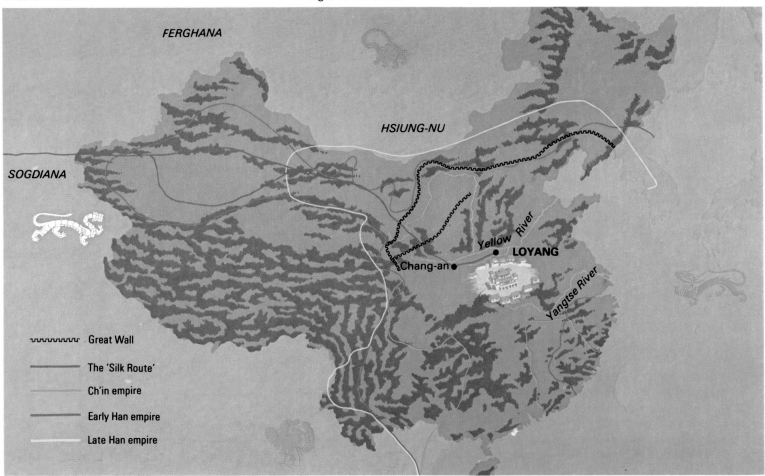

wwwwww Great Wall

——— The 'Silk Route'

——— Ch'in empire

——— Early Han empire

——— Late Han empire

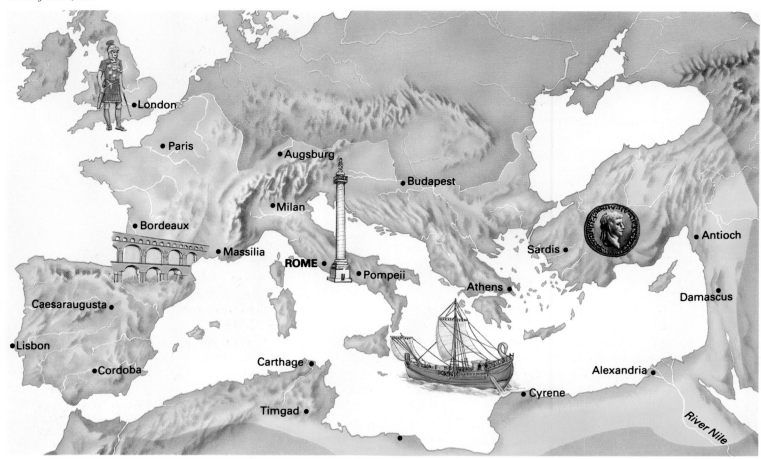

The Roman Empire in AD 117

Here, on this map, you can see the Roman Empire at the time of the Emperor Trajan's death in AD 117. This was its greatest extent; it comprised most of Western and Central Europe, all the Mediterranean and North African countries and a good part of Western Asia as far as the river Euphrates. The empire grew no larger because natural barriers, such as desert and mountains as well as more powerful enemies made further conquests unlikely and not worth the effort.

According to legend, Rome was founded in 753 BC by Romulus and Remus, but, in fact, it began as a small settlement of Latin farmers, ruled by the Etruscans, a gifted people who possibly came from Asia Minor. The Romans grew in numbers and aggressive spirit, until, by about 400 BC, they had overthrown the Etruscans and their own kings to become a republic governed by aristocrats called *patricians*. It took them another two hundred years of incessant wars to defeat all the various peoples of Italy, including the Greeks in the south, and to convert them into allies. During these wars, the common people of Rome (*plebeians*) managed to improve their position and win a bigger say in the government.

Then came the long struggle with Carthage, a powerful Phoenician trading colony of North Africa, in which not even the genius of the Carthaginian general, Hannibal, could overcome the Roman will to win. By the time Carthage was utterly destroyed (148 BC) Rome

had acquired Sicily, Sardinia, Corsica, Spain and much of North Africa; nor was it long before Greece itself was added to these possessions.

But the wars caused unemployment and misery in Italy, where from a savage struggle between the people's party, led by Julius Caesar, conqueror of Gaul, and the supporters of the Senate, Caesar emerged victorious. King in all but name, he began to rule well, but his enemies murdered him in 44 BC and it was left to his great-nephew Octavian, later called Caesar Augustus, to defeat all his opponents and make himself the first supreme head of state.

Thenceforward, Rome was ruled by an Emperor, whose power rested upon the army's support, while the huge empire, with its provinces inhabited by peoples of different races, religions and cultures, was managed by a civil service of governors, magistrates and officials.

Compared with the Ancient Egyptians, Greeks and Chinese, the Romans have had a bad press in recent years. People tend to remember their bloodthirsty games and wild beast shows, the wicked emperors and persecuted Christians and to forget the Romans' astonishing achievements. We ought to marvel at the efficiency of the men who ran the affairs of distant provinces, organized the building of towns, roads and waterways. They enforced law and order, encouraged education and enabled the peoples of many nationalities to live for two centuries in greater peace and security than any large area of the world had known before or, indeed, since the heyday of the Roman Empire.

The Roman Empire in AD 117. A Roman centurion, the aqueduct at Nîmes, Trajan's column in Rome, a bireme and a coin of Augustus Caesar indicate the extent of the Empire.

Ancient America

The ancient civilizations of America developed in complete isolation, for the peoples of Mexico and Peru had no idea that the Old World existed or that anyone else had built cities, temples, roads and irrigation systems.

Yet the first Americans had come in fact from the Old World, almost certainly via the Bering Strait about 12,000 years ago. They were hunters who made their way south and, when the glaciers retreated and big game became scarce or disappeared altogether, learned to live by food-gathering and then by growing crops, especially maize. By 1000 BC, when there were hundreds of farming villages in central Mexico and down the length of Peru, civilization was ready to emerge.

It began with the Olmecs, a mysterious people who inhabited Mexico's Gulf Coast and spread their influence and jaguar-worship throughout Middle America at about the same time as the Chavin people developed a similar culture in Peru. From these beginnings, three major civilizations arose: those of the Mayas, the Incas and the Aztecs.

The Mayas

The Mayas flourished from about AD 300 to 900 in Guatemala and Honduras, where they built majestic cities with mansions of carved stone and huge pyramid temples to an array of gods so numerous and terrifying that their priests held complete sway over the common people. They were able to read and write; they studied the stars and worked out a calendar and a system of arithmetic but, in about AD 900, their civilization collapsed. Perhaps the peasants overthrew the priest-rulers; at any rate, the jungle closed over the ruined cities, except in Yucatan, where the Mayas revived their building skills until they were conquered by the Toltecs of Mexico.

The Incas

Far to the south in Peru, the Incas built America's second great civilization in the fertile valleys of the Andes, where, from Cuzco, its capital, the Inca emperor exercised benevolent rule over many subject peoples. It was an empire linked by fine roads and a postal service, with an efficient government, industries and food-production. Astonishingly the Incas had no knowledge of iron, money or a written language.

In the 13th century, the Toltecs and Mayas were overcome by the Aztecs, energetic newcomers to Mexico, whose aggression made them masters of an empire of some 450 towns. It is their capital city, Tenochtitlan, which we shall explore later in this book.

Below, left: Location of America's ancient civilizations.
Right: Lake Texcoco, showing the position of Tenochtitlan. It is surrounded by symbols of the Aztec empire – two hairless dogs; the Golden mask of Xipe Totec, god of Fertility; the city's great temple; a warrior; and Xiuhtecuhtli, the Fire god. Although the town is in the tropics, its high altitude (2,250 metres above sea-level) gives it a mild healthy climate.

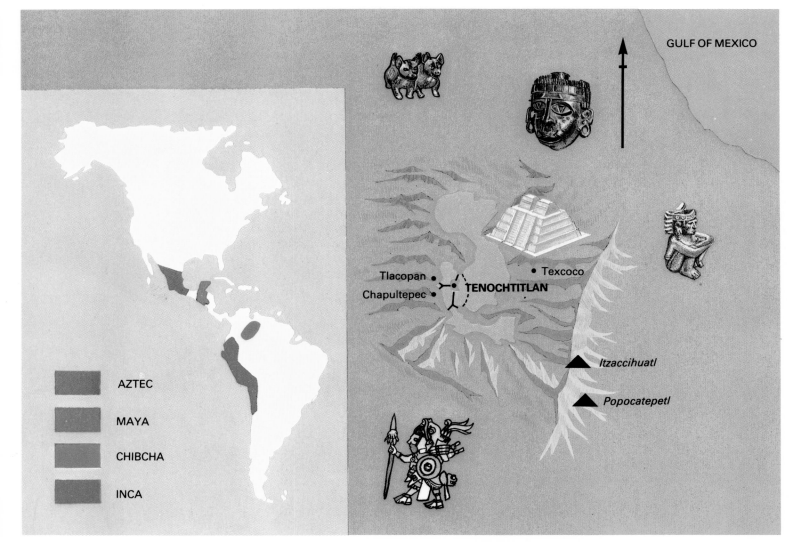

GULF OF MEXICO

Tlacopan
Chapultepec
TENOCHTITLAN
Texcoco

Itzaccihuatl

Popocatepetl

AZTEC

MAYA

CHIBCHA

INCA

Chapter Two

By the Banks of the Indus

In 1924, news came from India that an English archaeologist and his Indian colleagues had discovered remains of a civilization which seemed to be as old or nearly as old as those of Egypt and Sumeria. The picture on the right is a reconstruction of the city of Mohenjo-Daro, which once stood on the west bank of the Indus river. There and at Harappa, some 600 kilometres to the north-east, the excavations revealed hundreds of well-built brick houses and shops ranged along wide streets that were crossed by narrow lanes.

In the years up to the outbreak of the Second World War in 1939 and afterwards, more than a hundred other towns were discovered, most of them grouped round Mohenjo-Daro or round Harappa, the two largest cities which were separated by a stretch of barren desert. There was also a third group of towns around the Gulf of Cambay, one of which, called Lothal, appeared to be a port from which ships could have made ocean voyages.

The archaeologists had unearthed the Indus Valley or Harappan civilization which seems to have flourished for a thousand years, from about 2500 BC and occupied a million square kilometres, until it mysteriously collapsed and disappeared from history.

Among the finds were bathrooms and drainage systems, copper weapons and tools, household utensils, jewellery and pottery. On some of the pots, stone seals and baked clay tablets, there was writing. So far, no-one has managed to decipher the Indus script, so we know practically nothing about the rulers of this realm or its laws and history. What we do know is that Mohenjo-Daro and Harappa were far bigger than any of the other towns and must surely have been capital cities, though we can not tell if one was superior to the other or if both flourished at the same time.

The two capitals and the lesser towns were remarkably alike. On the western side, each had a citadel standing on an artificial mound and fortified by a brick wall and towers, apparently to protect the town's store of grain from robbers and flood waters. At Mohenjo-Daro, besides the Granary, there was also a Great Bath and a building that might have been an Assembly Hall. Below the citadel lay the lower town with its grid-plan of straight streets and baked brick houses.

Thus, although there are many gaps in our knowledge, there is enough information and evidence for us to try to put together a picture of life in the Indus Valley some 4000 years ago.

'This civilization is doubtless not as rich as those of Egypt and Mesopotamia, but the sites where it developed are characterized by an extraordinary skill in town planning.'
O. Viennot.

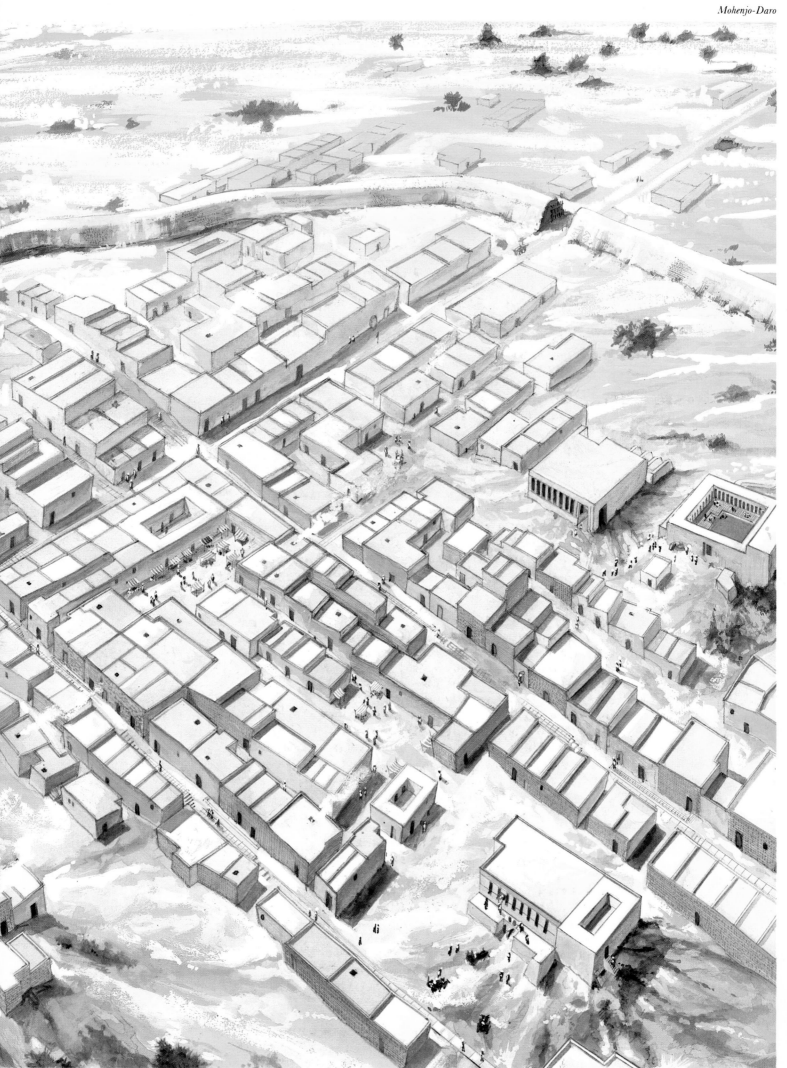

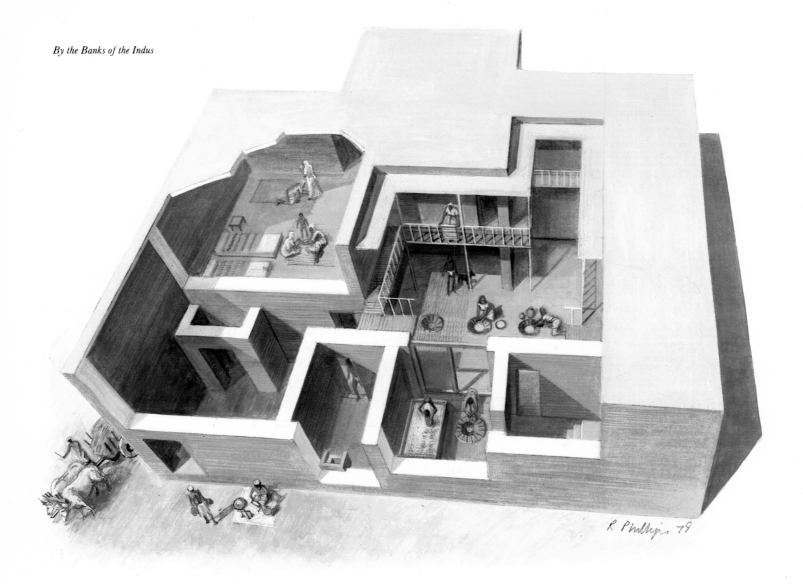

R Phillips 79

A House in Mohenjo-Daro

At Mohenjo-Daro, broad streets running north and south are crossed by others at right angles to divide the lower town into a number of blocks, each of which is subdivided by narrow lanes or alleys. Entrance doors to private houses are nearly always tucked away in these lanes, so the main streets are extraordinarily dull, for they present only blank walls to the passer-by. Nor are there many windows, because, in India's hot climate, it is important to try to keep rooms cool by allowing only the doorways to admit light and air. A small wooden or pottery grill is sometimes set up high in an outer wall to improve ventilation.

The houses, mostly two storeys high, are made almost entirely of burnt bricks, for there is little or no use for stone, even for pillars or decoration, but wooden beams are laid across to form the upper floors and the roof. The beams are spread with reed matting which is given a coating of clay, spread thickly and stamped or pounded to make a hard flat surface. Drain pipes carry away rain water.

Small houses open directly on to the street, but a visitor to a good-sized house like this one above is admitted into an entrance lobby or small court by the porter whose little lodge stands opposite the front door. A short passage leads into the main courtyard, which is open to the sky and is the centre of household activity, for this is where servants do most of the cooking, pound corn in a mortar surrounded by a circular brick platform and bake bread in the round oven in the corner.

The children play here and donkeys and oxen are sometimes tethered to a post beside their feeding bins. Some houses have extra wide doorways to admit pack-animals into the courtyard. On its near side is a small room containing the household well, with its brick coping raised a little above the floor and its platform for the water jars. This is also the bathroom, whose brick floor slopes towards one corner to allow water to run through an outlet into the adjoining lavatory or privy, which is fitted with a proper seat. An earthenware pipe runs under the floor of the bathroom and privy to connect with the main drain in the street outside, where manholes are set at intervals to permit inspection and cleaning.

A person taking a bath uses a clay scraper to remove dirt and sweat from his body; then he rubs scented oil into his skin. Sometimes a servant helps him.

From the courtyard, a brick staricase leads upstairs to the bedrooms and to the flat roof. Members of the family take their ease up here in the evenings and also spend the night during hot weather. Some large houses which are shared by several families have outside staircases to the various apartments.

Above: While the family relaxes at home, a man drives his oxen and cart laden with corn to the market.

Right: Both men and women work in the fields. Some tasks, such as sowing seeds, only women are allowed to do. A man raises water from a well by means of a *shaduf* (probably the world's oldest machine).

Working the Fields

On the citadel close to the Great Bath, stands the Granary, which, as you can see, consists of a massive brick base (or podium) with the timber-sided grain-store on top. Spaces have been left in the podium to allow air to circulate so that the grain will not go mouldy.

Ox-wagons laden with grain are backed into a bay from which sheaves of corn are hoisted up on to the unloading platform and thence into the storehouse.

This is one of the state granaries (there are twelve smaller ones at Harappa) which store the harvested corn from the city's fields, not solely to provide for the winter and to guard against floods, but also to provide wages for workers and officials because money is not used in the Indus Valley. Thus, in a way, the Granary serves as the Treasury.

With so many cities and towns to be supplied with food, farming has to be the chief occupation and, fortunately, the silt deposited by flood water produces excellent crops of wheat, barley, rice, peas and melons. Sesame and mustard are grown for their oil and cotton for making cloth.

On the left is a rice paddy-field, surrounded by mud banks to keep the water in. Rice-seedlings have to be lifted from their seed-bed and transplanted into these flooded plots by peasants working ankle-deep in mud. Alongside the adjoining plot, a man is raising water from a well by means of a *shaduf*, a counter-weighted beam on which a pot is hung. His helpers pour water into trenches running across the vegetable plot. (Unlike Mesopotamia, no traces of irrigation dykes and canals have been found in the Indus Valley. Centuries of alluvial deposits must have covered them, for, in a dry climate, it would have been impossible to produce enough food for the population without irrigation.)

Below the paddy-field, peasants are carrying out various jobs in the fields: a woman is using a foot plough which resembles a large spade, other women break up clods and a man tramples seeds into the soil. In the next scene, workers are harvesting grain with copper sickles and carrying sheaves away, possibly to a collection point from which they will be transported to the official Granary.

Indus farmers keep two kinds of cattle, the humped zebu seen here and an unhumped type; they also breed buffalo, sheep and pigs. Horses and donkeys are used for transport, as well as the oxen which draw solid-wheeled carts. (We have not included a picture of ploughing because there is virtually no evidence that ploughs were in use. However, some flint or quartz objects have been found which might have been ploughshares and common-sense suggests that a people who trained oxen to pull carts would readily invent a plough to make furrows in the soft alluvial soil.)

'Big cities with teeming populations like Harappa and Mohenjo-Daro could never have existed save in an agricultural country which was producing its own food on a large scale....'
Sir John Marshall, Director-General of Archaeology in India, January 14th 1928.

Reed Boats and Foreign Trade

This reed boat which these slaves are putting the finishing touches to, will shortly be sailing the seas towards the African continent to trade with the Sumerians.

Here you can see work going on in the dock area of Lothal, the Indus sea-port which is sited on the plain of Kathiawad, some 600 kilometres south of Mohenjo-Daro. A walled town, with a wharf and warehouses, its unique feature is a large dock, measuring about 225 x 37 metres, with a sluice gate at one end, from which ships sail up the Gulf of Cambay on trading voyages.

The ship in the foreground is being built of reeds harvested in vast quantities from the marshlands and tightly tied into bundles as thick as a man's leg or thicker and extended to any required length by lapping the ends of one bundle firmly into the end of another.

This is an imaginative picture, because we cannot be absolutely certain that ships were built in this way, but an amulet has been found with a carving of a ship with no mast, a sharp upturned prow and stern, similar in every way to the ships of ancient Egypt and Sumeria. A scratched picture on a piece of pottery shows a similar vessel, high at both ends but, instead of the cabin in the middle, it has a mast with two yardarms. This could well have been one of the sea-going ships which sailed along the Makran coast and up the Persian Gulf to trade with Sumerian cities like Eridu, Ur and Lagash.

We know from Mesopotamian documents that there was a good deal of trade between the Indus and Sumer; moreover Indus Valley seals, beads and other objects have been found in Mesopotamia, though hardly any Sumerian articles in the Indus Valley. This suggests that the Indus people bought mainly perishable goods such as barley, vegetable oils and cloth from the Sumerians. In their turn, the Sumerians probably bought valuable raw materials, such as copper, lead and gold.

The Indus people also traded overland with Susa in Persia and may have gone on from there to Mesopotamia. Their pack-animals were almost certainly donkeys, because there is hardly any evidence of camels in the Indus Valley at this time. For local transport, they made use of two- and four-wheeled carts, with solid wheels and a single shaft to which a pair of oxen could be yoked.

Craftsmen

The Indus craftsmen were certainly not as they were good potters accustomed to using a wheel and skilful metal-smiths who worked in gold and silver, copper and lead. They produced fine beads of semi-precious stones such as cornelian, agate and lapis lazuli, but their best work went into making stone seals, finely cut in attractive designs showing ox-like beasts with a single horn, elephants, rhinoceros, tigers and antelopes. These seals were probably used to stamp bales of merchandise with the owner's trade mark and name, though we cannot be sure of this until someone deciphers the Indus script. Their artists produced little terra-cotta figures of animals and humans, a few stone busts and bronze dancing-girls.

The Great Bath

Among the most important buildings in Mohenjo-Daro is the Great Bath, situated next to the Granary on the citadel. It measures about 27 x 13 metres and has a wide flight of steps leading down into the water. Its floor is made water-proof by a layer of bitumen (asphalt) underneath the bricks.

The Bath is enclosed by verandahs, behind which are rooms and, a short distance away, two groups of four bathrooms, each with a staircase leading to an upper room, which resembles a cell of a priest or monk.

The Great Bath, the cells and the large number of private bathrooms throughout the cities point to an exceptional love of cleanliness or to bathing as a religious rite, such as we can see being carried out in India today. It seems possible that the Indus people were governed by priest-rulers who lived in specially designed buildings (or 'colleges') on the citadels where they regularly washed or purified themselves in honour of the gods.

Their gods

Who were these gods? The many figurines of an almost nude woman suggest worship of a Mother Goddess, who made the land fertile and provided the world with food, young animals and children. Animals appear so frequently on seals that they too may have been gods with special powers, like those of ancient Egypt.

Unlike the Egyptians and Sumerians, the Indus people did not build grandiose temples to their gods or concern themselves about life after death and all the elaborate ceremonial of burying the dead with all kinds of possessions for use in the afterworld.

The Indus Civilization Collapses

In about 1500 BC, the Indus civilization collapsed and we do not know why. Some people think that the cities were destroyed by barbaric invaders, possibly by the Aryans. Certainly, there is evidence of a massacre at Mohenjo-Daro, but not elsewhere, so perhaps the Indus people brought about their own downfall by overcropping and over-grazing the land and by cutting down their trees for fuel to fire all those millions of bricks. Perhaps there were disastrous floods or a change of climate; the rainfall must once have been much heavier than in modern times, for the area which once supported thriving cities is now desert or arid scrub.

At all events, the Indus civilization vanished without trace for more than thirty centuries until it was rediscovered in the 1920s.

Bathers dry themselves in the changing rooms. In the foreground, is a fresh water well to replenish the pool and a brick drain down which runs excess or dirty water.

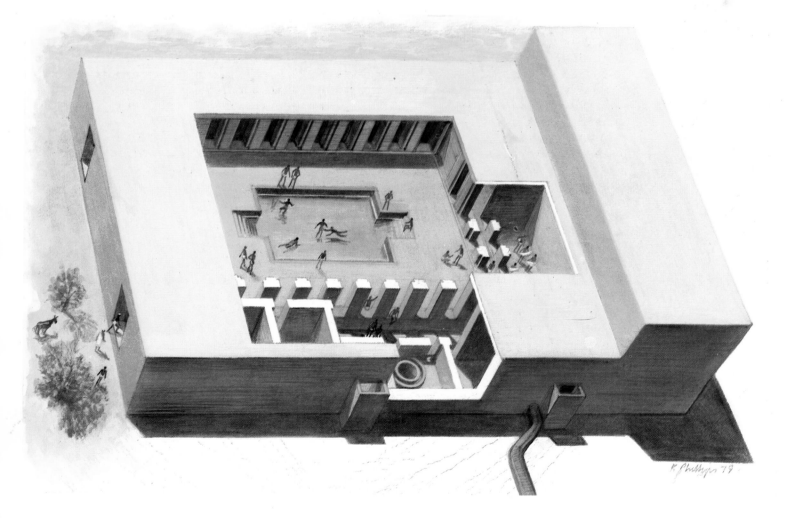

Chapter Three

A Town in Ancient Egypt

Here is a bird's eye view of the central part of the city of Akhetaten, where, for a brief while, the capital of the greatest empire in the world lay.

The city stood on the eastern bank of the Nile in Middle Egypt and was built to the orders of a Pharaoh who came to the throne as Amenhotep IV. He was the son of Amenhotep III, in whose reign Egypt reached her zenith of power and prosperity, when, at Thebes, Amen was the rich and apparently all-powerful state-god.

But Amenhotep IV, who became co-regent with his father in about 1386 BC, hated Amen, for he had come to believe that Aten, the sun-disk, was not merely greater than Amen and all the other gods, but was the *only* god. So, in order to worship Aten untroubled by the bitter hostility of the priests of Amen, he decided to leave Thebes and build a new capital 400 kilometres away to the north. It was to be called Akhetaten, meaning 'Horizon of the Aten', and, since his own name contained the hated name of Amen, he changed it to Akhenaten.

At a place where the cliffs curved away from the Nile to make a D-shaped sandy plain about 9 kms long by 4½ kms wide, the mushroom city rose at frantic speed, for Akhenaten and his wife, Nefertiti, urged the project on with all the fervour of religious maniacs. Much of the work was shoddy – rubble covered by a thin stone facing, mud-brick whitewashed to look like limestone – but workers were drafted to the site in such numbers that Akhenaten and his queen were able to take up residence within two years and, as far as we know, they never left their new capital for a single day.

Even if some of it was gimcrack, the city was laid out on spacious lines with broad streets and impressive buildings. Because of the importance of the Nile as a highway and source of water for canals and wells, the city had to be long and narrow, with the Main City in the centre, a North Suburb, and a North City, the South City and the lovely Palace of the Southern Pool. Out in the desert, between the city and the eastern cliffs, was a Workman's Village, which we shall describe later on. The tombs of the dead, so important to the Egyptians, were to be cut out of those eastern cliffs.

Gardens lined the green strip along by the river, though some of the large houses ran right to the water's edge. There were many wharves and mooring-places for the boats and rafts which not only brought supplies, but officials, workmen and foreigners from all parts of Egypt and its Empire to the new city. There was also the continuous coming and going of boats laden with produce from the farmlands on the west bank.

'They tremble when they behold the Nile in full flood. The fields laugh and the river banks are overflowed.'

The main areas and buildings in the central city, containing the temples, palaces and government offices:

1 King's Way
2 The Great Palace
3 King's House
4 The Bridge containing a window from which the King shows himself to his subjects
5 Main Hall
6 Coronation Hall
7 Royal Magazines, containing the treasure
8 Royal Temple
9 Great Temple
10 The Sanctuary
11 Slaughter House
12 North Suburb

A Nobleman's House

This nobleman's house on the corner of Straight Street in North Suburb, has been painstakingly reconstructed from the meagre ruins that were discovered some 3300 years after the city was abandoned (it was pretty well razed to the ground within 15 years of Akhenaten's death, when the priests of Amen recovered their power.)

Suppose you are visiting this house in its heyday. You go through the main entrance (1). Here the gatekeeper, whose lodge is on the left (2) checks who you are. You walk up a path leading to the family chapel (3) which contains an altar and a stele or upright stone with a carving of the King worshipping Aten. You enter the house via an inner courtyard and a porch whose doorway bears the owner's name; from the vestibule or lobby (4), a servant leads you into the North Loggia (5) – a kind of verandah – to greet your host who takes you into the Central Hall (6). The main living room has painted wooden pillars supporting the ceiling, a hearth with a brazier for cool evenings, a limestone slab where a servant will pour water over your hands and feet, and a raised dais where you seat yourself on a stool next to the master of the house. Smaller rooms lead off the Hall – the West Loggia (7), which is the winter sitting-room, and some guest bedrooms, the women's room (8) and the master's private suite, with his bedroom (9), bathroom (10) and lavatory. On the other side of the Hall, a door leads to a staircase which goes to the roof.

Outside the house are the gardens (17), with its trees, exotic shrubs and central pool, the household well (11), the cattle yard (15) and the kitchen (14), these last two placed at the south-eastern corner because the prevailing wind will carry away the smells. Along the southern walls are the servants quarters (13), the stables (12) and the chariot- and harness-room. A most important enclosure is the granary court (16), with four big corn-bins shaped like bee-hives in which wheat and barley are stored. These supply the household with bread and beer. In a country without coinage, grain is not only used for food and drink, but as a means of exchange; it is used to pay wages and taxes and to buy all kinds of goods.

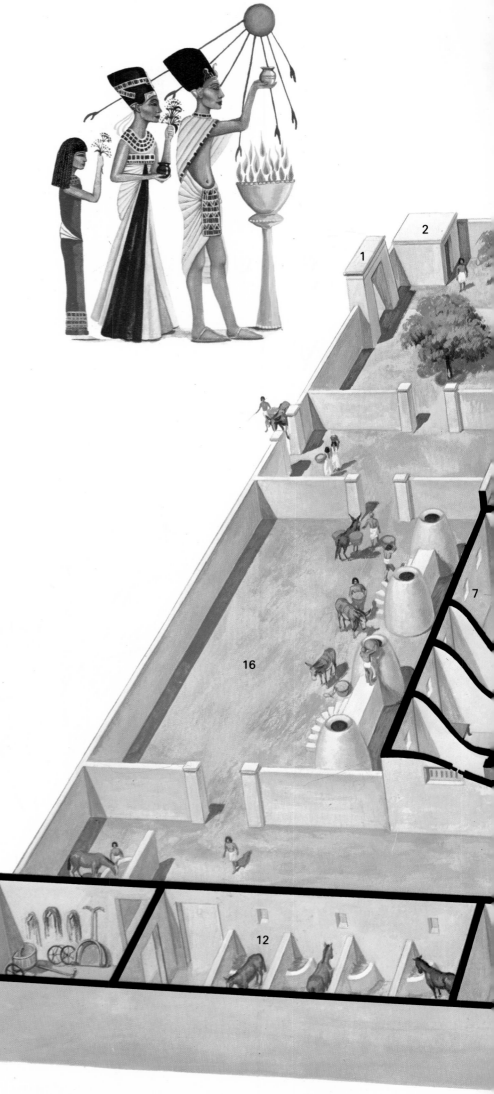

The inside of the house is decorated in bright colours, with painted beams and designs of rosettes, fruit and flowers. The decorations are not as sumptuous as those which adorn the walls of the tombs and the King's residence.

There is little furniture; it consists mainly of stools, chests, beds, small tables, wicker baskets and brightly coloured rugs and draperies. A few rugs and skins are spread on the tiled floors.

Far left: In the city built to honour Aten, much of its art records Akhenaten's devotion to the gods and here he is seen with Queen Nerfertiti and one of the princesses offering incense, fruit and flowers to the sun-disc, whose rays end in caressing hands.

Below: The house stands in extensive grounds, surrounded by a nine-metre high wall. Its plan is simple, for it consists of a central room whose walls extend higher than the rest of the house, so that clerestory or upper windows can be inserted to give this main room light and air. The smaller rooms are built all round the central one to keep it cool.

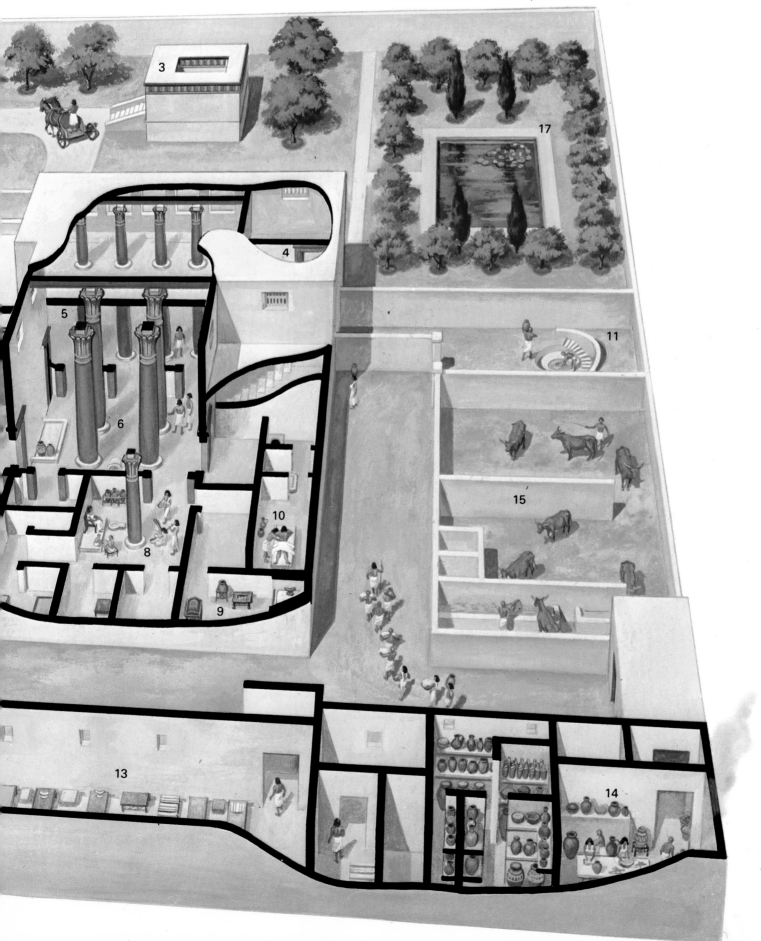

23

The Workmen's Village

Here is a construction of one of the most interesting sites ever excavated anywhere in the world. It is part of the Workmen's Village, set in the desert several miles to the east of the Southern City, a desolate spot so far from the river that every drop of water and morsel of food has to be transported by donkeys.

The village consists of 73 small houses, all alike in size and layout, built in terraces separated by five narrow lanes. There is just one larger house, which almost certainly belongs to the foreman or head gaoler, for the village is really a prison settlement surrounded by a high wall designed, not to keep enemies *out*, but to keep the inhabitants *in*. Beyond the wall is a road running all round on higher ground from which patrolling guards can keep watch on the village.

The Tombworkers

The men who live here with their wives and children are tombworkers. They are prisoners and criminals whom nobody wants in the gracious city of Akhetaten. Their task is to excavate and decorate tombs for important persons – work which fills normal people with dread. Although they have to labour for the honour and glory of Aten, they do not know much about this new god, for they cling to the old ones, especially their favourite, *Bes*, the little dwarf-god with a lion's face, a merry god who protects people against snakes and other terrors and helps women in child-birth.

Although their life is grim, toiling all day in the tombs and returning under armed escort to the village at dusk, the workers' houses are more comfortable than the slums of, say, Victorian Britain. Each cottage, five metres wide and ten metres deep, has four rooms and a useful roof-space. From the street, you go into the entrance hall which has a narrow window to admit light and a flight of steps leading up to the flat roof. An opening leads into the living-room, whose ceiling, higher than the rest of the house, is supported by a single column; behind this main room are the kitchen and bedroom.

Children usually sleep up on the roof, which is also their favourite playground, under a shelter made of matting on poles or in a little mud-brick room which their father has built on the roof. You can see two of these in the picture. Reed fences separate each family's roof-space from their neighbour's.

The outside walls of the houses are coated with mud-plaster but, inside, the rooms are usually white-washed or decorated in colour with materials filched from the tombs and the workmen sometimes add flower designs and even human figures.

In the lane outside, there are big water-jars and mangers for the domestic animals. The family cow or donkey is so valuable that it is usually brought into the house at night!

The entrance hall (1) contains a loom, tools and sometimes a manger for the goat or donkey; the floor is of sand or beaten mud.

In the living-room (2), you can see jars for water and beer, a low stool, a brick dais with rug and cushion, a storage-chest and a hearth for a charcoal fire. Notice the window-grill.

The kitchen (3), next to the bedroom with its low bed and neck-rest, contains the bread oven, pots, bowls and a mortar and pestle for grinding wheat into flour.

Building the City

From the outset, Akhenaten intended his new city to be the capital of the Empire, for he declared: 'The whole land shall come hither, for the beautiful seat of Akhetaten shall be another seat (capital) and I will give them audience whether they be north or south or west or east.'

The royal architect, Bek, designed three great temples for the god, one for the King himself, one for the queen-mother, Tiy, and one for the princess Beketaten, 'Maidservant of Aten'. In addition, there was the Great Palace, the King's residence, a Coronation Hall and many mansions for the favoured nobles who received grants of land from the monarch when the city was founded.

These great nobles and the leading officials took sites along the main roads of the central part of the city, leaving the inner spaces for less important people. Middle-class people – merchants and petty officials – mostly built their houses in the North Suburb, within easy reach of the Main City, while the workers put up their homes, many of them no better than hovels, on spare land which the others did not want and

often where they had dumped their rubbish.

Akhenaten, who has been depicted as a dreamy poet lost in adoration for his god while the Empire was crumbling under the attacks of its enemies, was in fact a young man of extraordinary drive and determination. Not only did he outface the powerful priests of Amen and have Amen's name hammered out of temples, statues and even from the top of lofty obelisks, but he put through this mammoth project of building a new and stylish capital at breakneck speed.

Building materials

Limestone, sandstone and alabaster for the temples had to be brought to the site from distant quarries. The timber came from abroad, chiefly from Lebanon, since Egypt's native trees produce no worthwhile timber for building.

However, the main needs were labour and vast quantities of building materials for the mansions, houses, workshops, wharves, warehouses and even hovels. Fortunately, Egypt possessed all of these in plenty. Ever since the days of pyramid-building, the peasants had been accustomed to being called up for forced labour on temple-construction

On the building site below, workmen are fetching water to be mixed with the mud by foot and hoe. Chopped straw is trodden in to improve the strength and binding quality. The brickmakers are said to 'strike' bricks when they lay them in rows to dry for two or three days. Labourers carry finished bricks to a half-built house on slings attached to a yoke balanced on one shoulder.

and irrigation projects and, thanks to the annual flood (the *Inundation*), there was a limitless supply of mud for bricks which could be baked outdoors in the hot sunshine.

Making bricks

Here we see workmen making mud-bricks on a building site. They use ordinary alluvial mud which they mix with water using hoes and their feet. They strengthen this rather pebbly paste by treading in chopped straw.

When the damp mass is thoroughly mixed, brick-makers pat the right amount of mud into wooden moulds and 'strike' their bricks, that is, set them out in rows on a level piece of ground to dry in the hot sun for two or three days.

By modern standards, the bricks are large – about 23 x 11 x 8 cms for houses and larger still, as much as 38 x 16 x 16 cms for the walls of palaces and forts. When they are thoroughly sun-baked, labourers carry them to the building point where the bricklayer lays them in courses at least two bricks thick with mortar between each course.

Mud bricks tend to dry unevenly and to shrink, so, to prevent the wall warping, the builder leaves the odd air-space between courses and, in the case of very big walls, inserts an occasional balk of timber which serves to 'tie' the bricks and to provide a certain amount of elasticity.

Egypt's building methods and the layout of towns and houses had much to do with its climate and geography. Towns had to be near the river because it was the main highway and the only source of water, yet they must not occupy the narrow fertile strip of land along its edge. We can see this clearly at Akhetaten. It was built on the desert, not too close to the fertile strip, but close enough to the Nile for wells to be sunk and, probably, for water channels to be dug.

Scarcity of rain allowed unfired mud bricks to be the almost universal material for every kind of building except the temples. These were built of stone because, as the home of gods, they were meant to last for ever. In such dry conditions, mud bricks had a very long life, for there was nothing to destroy them other than the wearing effect of wind-blown sand. To avoid this, the Egyptians plastered the surfaces of walls with mud. Even in the best houses, the only use of stone was for thresholds, doorways, lintels and circular bases for the wooden pillars which supported ceilings. We have already noted how houses were planned to take advantage of the prevailing north wind and to keep the central room as cool as possible.

In crowded towns like Thebes and even in some villages where land was scarce, houses were built two and three storeys high. But where there was ample space, as at Akhetaten, the rich were able to enjoy living in their ideal house – a spacious one-storey dwelling with verandahs and open courts surrounded by gardens.

Muscle-power

It would have been impossible to build the new capital so speedily without the system of forced labour which everybody, except priests and officials, was conscripted to carry out for the state. In practice, forced labour fell upon the peasants and artisans who were called upon to leave their villages and work for weeks and even months in the gangs that erected temples and palaces.

The workers received wages in the form of bread, vegetables, dried fish and beer, with an occasional bonus issue of clothing, wine and body oils. On long-term projects, such as the building of Akhetaten and the excavation of the royal tombs in the Valley of the Kings, the workers were given permanent houses, like those in the Workmen's Village.

Akhenaten's temples and palaces were raised by muscle-power, for the Egyptians never invented the pulley or scaffolding, but relied upon the strength of the workers and their skilful use of levers and rollers to move huge blocks of stone. As a building grew higher, there rose with it an earth ramp up which the blocks were hauled into position; when it was completed, it could be decorated from the top downwards by gradually removing the ramp until it was finally cleared away.

'All the houses except one, the overseer's, were of the same size and built precisely on the same plan.'
C. Leonard Woolley,
May 6th 1922.

The Tomb of Aahmes

This is a see-through section of one of the tombs in the cliffs which rise up from the desert east of the city and which you can visit today, reaching the site by donkey, tractor or truck. In his devotion to the new religion, Akhenaten did not forget his supporters' profound belief in a life after death and in the absolute necessity for a man to have his body preserved and placed in a safely hidden tomb furnished with provisions and all kinds of objects which he would need in the next world.

The King, therefore, as an honour, presented his leading officials with sites for their tombs which were excavated by gangs from the Workmen's Village. As in the city itself, the work was carried out in a furious hurry; many of the tombs were never finished, for no sooner had the quarriers started on one than they were called away to begin another. The draughtsmen and artists would come in to outline their pictures and decorate as much of the walls as had been completed before they, in their turn, had to start another job. Then the quarriers might come back. . . .

In plan, the tombs are similar to one another. From a forecourt, you enter a large Hall cut out of the solid rock. Its roof is usually supported by pillars of rock and the walls decorated with vivid pictures. The scenes are in *low relief*, that is, the artist has cut away the background so that the horses, chariots, people and so on stand out a little from the wall and can be completed in bright colours made from natural pigments, such as red ochre, chalk and soot. Finally, the whole is sealed with a coating of beeswax or varnish.

Beyond the Hall, a corridor is cut at right-angles and decorated with more scenes and, opposite, is the shrine (2) containing a statue of the dead man. From the Hall, a grave shaft has been cut to reach the burial chamber (1) in which the mummified body will rest.

In our tomb, almost certainly that of Aahmes, the Royal Fan-bearer, nearly all the pictures show the King basking in the rays of Aten, riding in his chariot with the Queen, making offerings and sitting at ease with his family. Aahmes is there, serving his royal master, as he will continue to do, presumably, in the after-life.

These wall-paintings are very important because, just in case all the possessions and even the mummy are stolen or destroyed, the scenes of everyday life will, by magic, still enable Aahmes' spirit to live on for ever.

In fact, all the tombs have been badly damaged, first by supporters of Amen who came to destroy every trace of the hated religion, next by robbers who removed whole sections of paintings in order to sell them to museums and lastly by local people who, from fear or superstition, cut out some of the faces in order to kill those persons' spirits.

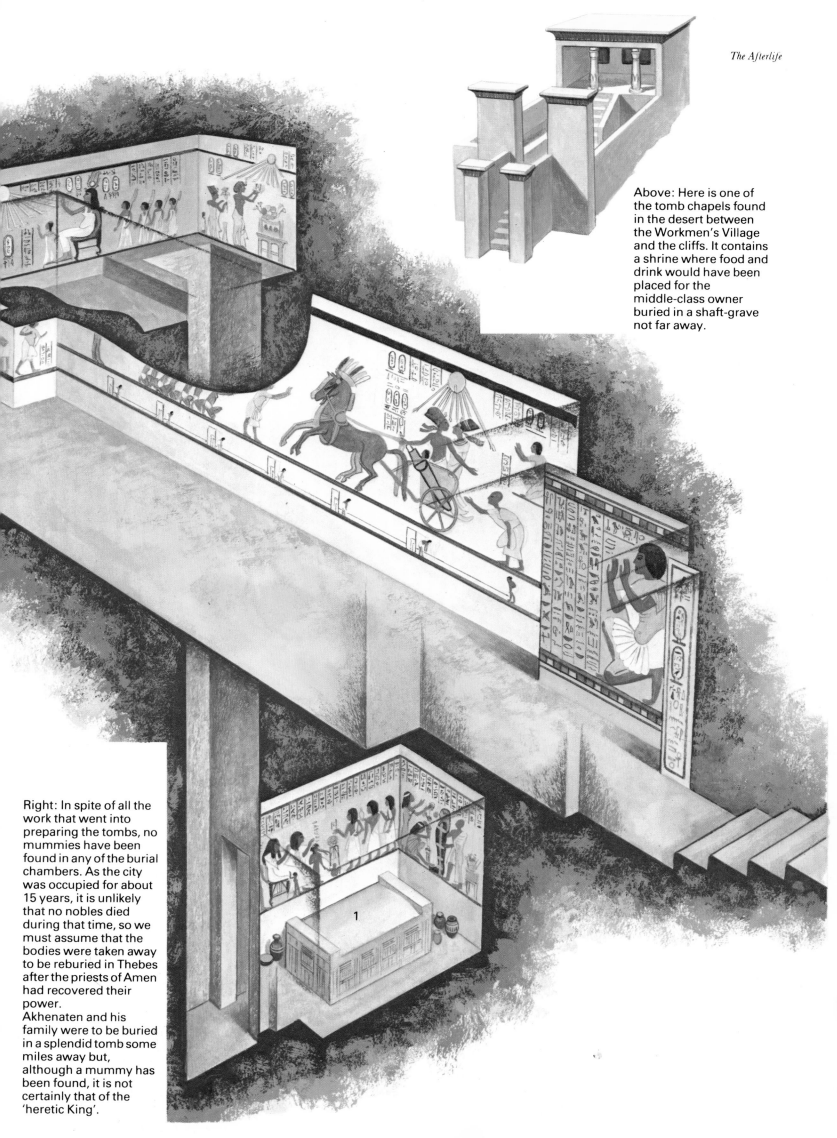

Above: Here is one of the tomb chapels found in the desert between the Workmen's Village and the cliffs. It contains a shrine where food and drink would have been placed for the middle-class owner buried in a shaft-grave not far away.

Right: In spite of all the work that went into preparing the tombs, no mummies have been found in any of the burial chambers. As the city was occupied for about 15 years, it is unlikely that no nobles died during that time, so we must assume that the bodies were taken away to be reburied in Thebes after the priests of Amen had recovered their power.
Akhenaten and his family were to be buried in a splendid tomb some miles away but, although a mummy has been found, it is not certainly that of the 'heretic King'.

Chapter Four

Nebuchadnezzar's Babylon

For a century, until about 2000 BC, the city of Ur was the dominant power in the rich Tigris-Euphrates valley of Sumeria, until its ruling dynasty was overthrown by invaders from the mountains and the Arabian desert. Among them was a tribe – the Amorites – who seized a little town on the Euphrates called Babylon and made it the capital of the kingdom of Babylonia, which the great Hammurabi (1792-1750 BC) ruled with remarkable vigour and justice.

But a land so rich and fertile attracted yet more invaders. They overthrew Babylonia and occupied the valley until there emerged one race more ferocious and brilliantly successful in war than all the rest. They were Assyrians who, between 1350 and 612 BC, established, by conquest, the largest empire that the world had so far known. At one time, it included Egypt itself but dramatically and suddenly it collapsed, in the face of the continued assaults by the Medes and the Chaldeans.

The remnants of the Assyrian empire were seized by a Chaldean King, whose son, Nebuchadnezzar II (604-561 BC), rebuilt Babylon in such fabulous splendour that it came to be regarded as one of the wonders of the world.

The city stands mostly on the eastern bank of the Euphrates, with an extension called the 'New Town' on the western bank. Beyond its walls, stretches a green belt of palm trees and cultivated fields, for the Babylonians have long since mastered the technique of irrigation.

All round the city runs a massive rampart, consisting of two thick walls, some 12 metres apart, with the space between filled with rubble to make a roadway along which troops and chariots can dash to repel an attack. These defences are strengthened by a wide moat, crossed by bridges to the city's eight gates.

From the 'New Town', you cross a fine bridge over the Euphrates to reach the Processional Way, a paved thoroughfare which runs along the walled side of a vast precinct, whose pyramid-temple or *ziggurat* towers over the city. To your right, is another temple to the god Marduk; then the Processional Way turns left and runs due north for nearly 1000 metres to the magnificent Ishtar Gate, just beyond the Royal Palace, which has five courtyards and a lofty building so cunningly adorned with flowers, trees and shrubs that it is called the Hanging Gardens of Babylon.

Beyond the Ishtar Gate, Nebuchadnezzar has built himself another palace protected by strong walls and, elsewhere in the city, we find a number of temples to various gods, residential districts of private houses, which are flat-roofed and built around one or more courtyards.

'They drank the wine and praised the gods of gold, and of silver, of brass, of iron and of stone.'
Daniel.

R Phillips 79

A House in Babylon

As in most Eastern countries, a Babylonian house is built round a central courtyard, and because the owner wants privacy and relief from the burning sun, there are no windows facing on to the street, only a door, guarded by a trusty slave, who admits visitors and takes delivery of oil, barley or any other goods, which he carries to the store-room.

You cannot peep into the courtyard from the street but have to take a right-angle turn to reach the central part of the house. Here the children play games and slave women rub out grain on a stone in order to make the crisp barley loaves which everyone eats. The kitchen, to the right of the courtyard, contains the cooking hearth consisting of two brick platforms with a space between for a charcoal fire and a narrow slit at the top where pots and pans can be placed. There are also big water jars which the slaves fill at the riverside, storage jars for beer, wine, grain and oil and various pottery bowls and basins. The slaves (two or three to the average household) sleep on this side of the courtyard.

The principal living-room is furnished with woollen rugs, a table and several wooden seats with plaited rush seats. If they can afford to do so, Babylonians like to live well, taking a substantial breakfast at dawn, a light lunch followed by a sleep, a main evening meal and a snack at bedtime. Meals consist chiefly of vegetables, fruit and a kind of barley gruel. Meat, such as beef, mutton and goat-meat, is mainly for the well-to-do. At times, the rich indulge in a duck or a brace of pigeons boiled in a stew. The Euphrates abounds in fish and although pigs are despised as street-scavengers, pork is often eaten by poorer families.

The Shrine

One room contains a shrine to the household gods and, beneath it, a deep brick-lined shaft in which the dead are placed, thus preserving the family unity. In the bathroom, the brick floor slopes towards the centre so that water, poured by a slave over his seated master, runs down into a sump and runs out into the street via upright earthenware pipes. This also serves as a drain for the lavatory and kitchen.

Some houses are all on one level, but others have a staircase leading to an upper floor, with a balcony off which are several bedrooms, furnished simply with divan-type beds, a stool or two chests made of terracotta or wood for storing clothes.

Throughout the house, ceilings and walls are whitewashed, for Babylonians believe it is unlucky to use bright colours indoors. Floors are usually made of brick and sometimes waterproofed by coating it with bitumen. The roof is made of palm-wood timbers, overlaid with reed matting. The whole is covered with a thick layer of mud.

Hammurabi (c1792-1750 BC), possibly the greatest ruler of ancient times, was the sixth of the Amorite Kings. His ancestors had led their people into the Euphrates valley. A mighty warrior, he fought the Elamites for 30 years, drove them out and, as lord of the whole plain, devoted the rest of his life to bringing order and system to his kingdom. His Code of Laws, engraved on a pillar in Marduk's temple, were remarkably advanced and humane, for they not only regulated justice, education, business and standards of workmanship, but they gave legal rights to women and slaves.

Below: One of the Seven Wonders of the World, the Hanging Gardens of Babylon inspire wonder in the minds of the Babylonian sailors gliding towards home on the outskirts of the city.

The Hanging Gardens

In the north-east corner of the grounds of the Royal Palace, not far from the Ishtar Gate, stands a most remarkable building raised up on an immensely strong foundation of arched vaults to form a series of terraces which you can see rising above the palace outer wall to a height of 23 metres.

This great structure, mostly made of brick, is faced with hewn stone, a material so costly in Babylonia that it appears hardly anywhere else in the city, and the terraces have been water-proofed with bitumen and lead and finally covered with layers of earth deep enough to support numbers of quite large trees. In ad-dition to trees, the terraces are planted with exotic shrubs, ferns and trailing plants which, in the flowering season, spread into a profusion of such brilliant blossoms that the building is known as the Hanging Gardens of Babylon.

King Nebuchadnezzar is said to have built this masterpiece to please one of his wives, a Persian princess who, in this flat desert, pined for the mountains and colours of her native country. On each side of the flight of steps leading to the uppermost terrace stands a colossal statue of a winged lion with the head of a bearded man, wearing a headdress with horns to indicate that he is a god. The custom of guarding the entrance to a temple or palace with huge figures of animals is a very old one in Sumeria. These human-headed lions and bulls were introduced by the Assyrians to keep away evil spirits.

The Hanging Gardens need a constant supply of water which is brought from the Euphrates and raised to a reservoir by means of an irrigation machine, either a screw or an end-less chain of buckets kept moving by slaves. The river, which runs right by the palace wall, is very busy and carries a great deal of shipping. It serves as a main highway for trade, with reed boats from northern states bringing copper, iron and alum down to the capital, while foreign ships arrive from the Persian Gulf carrying im-ports such as spices and gold.

The tall *ziggurat* in the background is the temple of Ninmah, the Great Mother and goddess of the underworld.

R. Phillips 79

The Ishtar Gate

The northern entrance to the world's most magnificent city is guarded by the Ishtar Gate, a strongpoint of breath-taking splendour which is approached by a broad processional way paved with limestone slabs bordered by blocks of marble. This highway runs upwards towards the Gate between high glazed walls decorated with figures of lions in enamelled brick, some white with yellow manes, some yellow with red manes. Each is about two metres long and set on a blue background so they advance, snarling to scare away evil spirits, to meet the traveller. There are 120 of these splendid animals, 60 on each side of the roadway.

The Ishtar Gate really consists of two gateways, because the city is protected by a double wall; the outer gate – an arch flanked by battlemented towers – is connected to the inner gate which is considerably higher. This huge entrance is covered with shining blue glaze, adorned with figures of bulls and dragons in alternate rows and arranged so that they come towards the arriving visitor. In the chamber connecting the two gateways, they face the entrance, while, on the walls of the towers and arch, they look inwards. Altogether, six rows of these animals are visible, each about one metre high, making 357 in all, and there are more rows beneath the road level, since it has had to be raised several times.

The realistic bulls and the curious dragons, with their serpent heads, cat-like bodies, lion's front paws and eagle's talons on the back legs, are in yellow and white on a blue background, while at pavement level there is a pretty border.

Every year, in the month of Nisan (March), the New Year's Festival is held to celebrate the marriage of Marduk with the Earth Goddess, which will bring fertility to the soil and a good harvest in the irrigated fields. The festival lasts for eleven days, during which all kinds of prayers, offerings and ablutions take place, until, on the sixth day, some lesser gods arrive from other cities to visit Marduk, including his son, Nabu.

Next, a great procession leaves the temple to pass through the Ishtar Gate, with the King, priests and statues of the gods riding in their ceremonial wagons as they make their way, if necessary partly by barge, to the *Akitu-house*, a temple outside the city. Later, after ceremonies to bless the fields, they return by the same route along the Processional Way accompanied by rejoicing crowds, to restore Marduk's image to its resting-place in the *cella* of his temple by the *ziggurat*.

Ishtar, after whom the fabulous gateway is named, is the chief goddess of Babylonia, greatly honoured and respected, since she is the goddess of love, motherhood and, strangely, war. Her image is carried before the army into battle and, yet, as both the Morning Star and the Evening Star, she brings love, fertility and growth.

'I am Nebuchadnezzar, King of Babylonia. I paved the way of Babel with stones, for the procession of the great lord Marduk. Marduk, lord, give eternal life.' Inscription on the underside of each marble paving stone lining Procession Street.

Religion

Like Egyptians, Greeks and Romans, Babylonians believe in a great many gods and evil spirits. Every town and village has its own deity; every family looks to its household gods for protection and no-one would dare to cast aside the ancient gods of Sumeria, who include Anu, god of the sky, Shamash, the sun, En-lil, a very powerful god, and the goddess of fertility who is called Ninmah or Ninursag. There are also Sin, the moon god, Nin-gal or Nanna, the moon goddess and a host of demons. Finally, the great Hammurabi decreed that Babylon's local god, Marduk, should become the supreme god or *Bel*, so he is often called Bel-Marduk.

Son of Ea, Marduk is the Sun-god, the King of Heaven and Earth, 'the god who creates everything' and also the god of magic. His wife is Zarpanit or Sarpanitum, a powerful goddess, which means: 'brilliant as silver who shines resplendent among the stars'.

The Ziggurat

Approaching Babylon by river or across the plain, a traveller first sees what seems to be a small mountain rising high above the city walls. This is the immense temple-tower or *ziggurat* which King Nebuchadnezzar has built in Marduk's honour. This mighty edifice (see p.30) rises in seven terraces to form a pyramid taller than the pyramids of Egypt; at its top stands the Holy of Holies, the little shrine, roofed with pure gold, which is sacred to Marduk and his wife, Zarpanit. A great staircase leads up to the second stage, beyond which smaller flights of steps encircle the building to enable the priests, but no-one else, to reach the shrine.

The ziggurat's core is a colossal mass of rubble, the remains of earlier ziggurats, and the whole structure is faced with bricks, some glazed in brilliant blue. Within the walled *timenos* or temple area, are the priests' quarters, storehouses for the god's accumulated wealth, courts and lesser temples where ordinary people make their offerings.

Downfall

The wealth which enabled Nebuchadnezzar to build in such dazzling style came partly from loot which his father won from the Assyrians and partly from his own campaigns in which he defeated the Egyptians, sacked Jerusalem and won possession of the thriving seaports along the Phoenician coast. He also increased Babylon's trade with the west.

But, in Babylonia, a great part of the land was owned by the temples, whose high priests amassed enormous wealth for Marduk from rents, tithes, river-tolls, taxes and successful trading missions. The King took as big a share of these revenues as he could lay hands on but the priesthood was too powerful to overthrow and the cost of his wars and vast building schemes produced such inflation and famine that within a few years of his death, Babylon had become so weak that the glorious city fell to Cyrus the Persian without a struggle.

The New Year procession going through the great Ishtar Gate into the city of Babylon. This is one of eight gateways into the city and was excavated by German archaelologists in 1913.

35

Chapter Five

A Greek 'City-State'

The town here is Priene. It was built in 600 BC or a little later, not in what is now Greece, but on the west coast of Asia Minor, not far from Miletus.

From the early days of city-states – such as Athens and Corinth – Greeks left their mainland homes when the population increased and food ran short, to found *colonies* overseas; in Sicily, for example, and along the shores of the Black Sea and especially, like Priene, in Asia Minor. They still felt themselves to be Greeks, and Priene is not only thoroughly Greek in spirit and culture but is also a good example of town-planning.

'At the crack of dawn when the cock crows, everybody awakes and sets off to work: the metal-smith, the flour-maker, the tanner, the shield-maker and the bath-man. They all dress in a hurry and set off while it is still dark.'
Aristophanes
5th century BC.

1 The Agora
2 Temples
3 Council Hall or *bouleuterion*
4 Theatre
5 Gymnasia
6 Stadium

5

The Greeks chose the site for their new town carefully. There had to be a rocky hill, easy to defend on which to build an *acropolis* (it is just off the top of the picture), a good water supply, access to the sea and cultivatable farmland. The town was laid out on a grid-plan, with broad streets crossing narrower ones more or less at right angles to divide the town into blocks.

The large open space in the centre is the *agora* or market-place; close by are several important civic buildings – temples, the Council House, a gymnasium and a fine open-air theatre. In the foreground is the *stadium* or running-track, and another gymnasium. A strong defensive wall runs all round the town.

The Town Centre

This big open space is the *agora*, the heart of Priene and the centre of all its important activities. But, first and foremost, it is the market-place where peasants from the surrounding countryside set up their stalls to sell fruit, vegetables, chickens, honey and eggs to the slaves who come to buy produce for their masters' households. All kinds of other goods, such as pots, bronze-ware, textiles, sandals and goats are on sale and there is another market alongside for fish and meat. Foreign traders come here to do business with Greek merchants.

Towards one end of the agora is an altar and, at the sides, several statues of gods and prominent citizens. At the bottom left of the agora is a roofed fountain where women fill their jars with water brought from the town spring in underground pipes.

Stoas

Along the sides of the agora run open colonnades, called *stoas*, which provide covered walks useful both in hot weather and in the winter for people to perambulate, meet one another and do business. In the colonnades are all kinds of shops, money-lenders' stalls and the offices of lawyers and magistrates. Here you will see a schoolmaster teaching a class of boys seated around him on the tiled floor and, over there, a philosopher strides up and down explaining his ideas to a group of students.

The agora is also the place where religious ceremonies are held and where all official proclamations of the Council are made. There are no newspapers, so this is where people come to hear the latest news and gossip, to listen to political speakers and to argue with one another about how the town should be run.

The Council House

Since this is the town centre, most of the important buildings are nearby; the building with an altar in the centre and men seated in rising tiers is the Council House where local affairs are debated. In practice, the town is run by a group of rich and important men, but every free-born citizen (though not women, foreigners or slaves) has the right to go and have his say in the Assembly.

Temples

There are several temples in Priene. A particularly fine one is dedicated to the goddess Athene. The temple dedicated to Asclepius, the god of healing, really serves much the same purpose as a hospital. In the fields just outside the built-up part of the town stands the temple of Demeter, the corn-goddess and much-loved earth-mother.

In the market-place, money has taken the place of barter. The chief Greek coin is the *drachma*, which weighs 4 to 7 grams and is divided into 6 *obols*. Higher units are the *stater* (2 drachmas), the *talent* (60) and the *mina* (100). Coins are normally of silver and Athenian money is the most reliable.

The only animal in the agora is a donkey laden with panniers; there are no vehicles. The Greeks possess two-wheeled carts but make more use of pack-animals and porters.

PRIENE

Priene was one of the Ionian city-states (Ionia was the name given to the coastal strip of Asia Minor) which banded together in a League for common defence; they generally looked to Athens for support. As Priene only had about 4000 inhabitants, it kept on good terms with Miletus, the rich maritime city just to the north, but it was strong enough to contribute 12 ships to the Ionian fleet which was defeated by the Persians in 494 BC. A prominent citizen Bias of Priene, had earlier suggested that all the Ionians should migrate to Sardinia, advice which, if taken, would have saved them from slavery.

A Greek House

In Priene, as in many places with a sunny climate, a house is usually built round a court-yard, which you enter from the dusty side-street; this one has a shrine in the middle, a colonnade all round and a flight of steps leading to the upper rooms. In many houses, the court-yard has an *impluvium* or shallow pool to catch rainwater from the roofs above. The front part of the house is taken up by a large storeroom, the porter's lodge and a shop, whose separate entrance you passed in the street. It is let to a man who sells pots, bowls, wine-jars and black vases. These are exquisitely decorated with figures drawn in thin red lines of men, women, warriors, gods and animals.

The main part of the house is beyond the courtyard and the cool porch or verandah, from which you can see the womenfolk preparing a meal in the kitchen where they cook over a charcoal fire on a raised hearth. Next to the kitchen is the bathroom and, often, an indoor privy, and next again the winter sitting-room, warmed if need be by a fire in a brazier.

To the left of the kitchen is the best room in the house, the *andron*, or dining-room, with its painted walls and fine mosaic floor. Here the master dines with his male friends, all reclining on their elbows, as they eat from low tables and spend hours drinking wine and discussing poli-tics, philosophy and sport. Apart from these dinner-parties, men spend little time at home, for they prefer to meet their friends outdoors in the street and the agora or in the gymnasium; in their opinion, home is for women and children, a place in which to eat and sleep. This is a men's world, in which women have practically no part to play outside the home.

Upstairs are bedrooms and the women's workroom, where you can see two girls spinning and weaving. Though not plentiful, furniture is well-made in simple graceful styles; it consists mainly of the men's dining couches, beds, a few stools and low tables, chairs with plaited-thong seats and some chests and baskets for storing clothes and household linen; the women possess various small boxes for their jewellery and beauty aids.

Most town houses were built on a stone base, although some had plain earth walls. The walls were made of mud bricks, and the upper floor and roof were held up by wooden beams. The mud bricks were not baked. They were very soft, and so were easily cut through by burglars – who were known as *toichorychoi,* 'wall-diggers'.

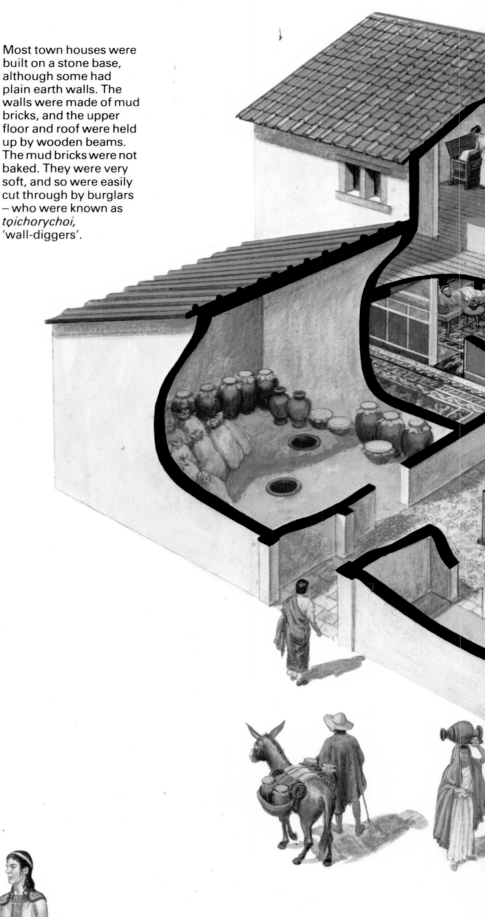

Left: Greek women usually wear a loose dress called a *chiton* in either the Dorian style (far left), with its deep-folded top, or the Ionian style (middle) which has no fold but is pinned or sewn along the arms and gathered at the waist by a girdle. The woman on the right is wearing a *peplos*, a woollen tunic-like dress with a high belted waist. In cool weather and out of doors, they wear a loosely-draped shawl called the *himation.*

Above: Men wear either the short *chiton,* a tunic which leaves the right shoulder bare for work or battle, or a long loose robe, pleated and made of linen. There are two kinds of cloaks: a smaller one, folded double over the shoulder and the large *himation*. Although men usually go bare-headed, they sometimes sport a funny little hat with turned-up brim or the peasant's floppy sun-hat.

41

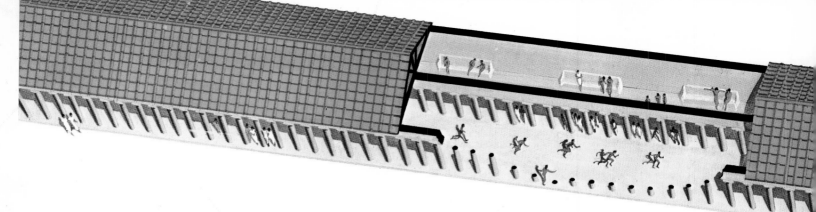

School and Sport

Sport is tremendously important, partly because it trains young men to become warriors and also because the Greeks admire physical strength and athletic skill. So they provide sports centres, *gymnasia*. These buildings have changing-rooms, wash-rooms and other facilities surrounding the exercise-ground with a sandy floor. This open space, called the *palaestra*, is first and foremost for training wrestlers, because wrestling and running are the most highly-prized sports, but it is also used for practising throwing the discus and javelin, long-jump, boxing, in which no gloves are used but the fighters bind their hands with thongs, and the *pankration*, which combines boxing, all-in wrestling and kicking!

The athletes train hard and often practise running and jumping with weights in their hands to improve performance. They are also careful to make prayers and offerings to the gods in whose honour sports festivals are held.

Attached to the gymnasium is a covered running-track, called the *dromos* (above), intended mainly to train sprinters for competitions between rival gymnasia and cities. These are held at the *Stadium* (see p.36), a track one *stade* long (about 200 metres) with banks of seats on either side for spectators. A race is generally of one stade, but there are longer ones of two, four and even 24 stades. Special events, such as chariot-racing are also held.

The athletes wear no clothes, for they take great pride in their muscular bodies and laugh at foreigners who are taken aback to see them racing naked. Prizes are seldom valuable – just a wreath of wild olive or a flask of oil – since competitors are there to honour the gods or their own city. Nevertheless, a famous athlete is a public hero, acclaimed wherever he goes and rewarded by his own people with gifts and servants at the public expense.

On arrival at the gymnasium (bottom right), the athletes leave their *chitons* in the care of a slave in the changing-room, oil themselves all over and add a coating of fine sand if they are going to wrestle, for this gives a better grip. After a hard training-session, they scrape the dust and sweat off with a curved scraper, take a bath and lie on a slab for massage and oiling.

The four greatest festivals are the Pythean, Isthmian, Nemian and, above all the Olympic Games. For the last, held every four years in honour of Zeus, a truce is declared so that athletes and spectators can come in peace from

---

SCHOOL

In Ancient Greece, boys were trained to use both their brains and their bodies, so they went to school and, later, to the big public *gymnasia*. In this school, below, the boys are writing with a sharp instrument on a wooden tablet covered with wax; when the master has corrected an exercise, the wax is smoothed over and used again. Pupils have to learn long passages of poetry, mostly by Homer, which they recite aloud and they also learn to do sums and a special sort of dancing, rather like ballet or mime. Music is important because a gentleman is expected to be able to sing and accompany himself on a lyre, the seven-stringed harp on which you can see the boys practising.

Below: Before they can write, these little boys have to learn their alphabet, which begins with the first two letters – *alpha, beta.* The old men in the background are special slaves, known as pedagogues, whose morning job is to take their young masters to school — perhaps to make sure they don't play truant!

all over Greece and wherever Greeks have settled overseas to the plain at Olympia. The Games last for five days, during which the greatest event is the Pentathlon in which each athlete competes in five sports – running, jumping, discus, javelin and wrestling – and the olive wreath goes to the man judged to be the best all-rounder. Other events include boxing, the pankration, races for chariots and mounted horses, contests for boys, musical performances and poetry recitals. (The Marathon race is not part of the Olympic Games.)

This gymnasium caters for every sport from boxing and wrestling to ball games, swimming and long jump. By the *dromos* (above left), the teachers encourage the young athletes.

The Temple

In the inner sanctum or *cella* of this splendid temple is the statue of a goddess, probably Athena, who is clad in an embroidered robe and attended by her priests and priestesses who proffer gifts but do not allow ordinary mortals to enter.

Sacrifice to the goddess takes place outside in the open air, where worshippers, mostly clad in white, wearing wreaths and carrying offerings of fruit, cereals, cakes and wine, approach an altar on which the head priest has lit a fire. A white ox, its head wreathed with flowers, is led forward to be stunned by an axe; its throat is cut so that the blood spills on the altar and, after its entrails have been burnt in the fire, the rest of the carcase will be roasted to provide a sacrificial feast for the worshippers.

The Greeks being practical people expect the gods to grant them favours in return for the sacrifices and offerings – success in the Games, a good harvest and so on. For very important matters, such as going to war, they may consult the Oracle at Delphi, a priestess who foretells the will of the gods.

The Greeks believe in scores of gods, from the most important ones, the Olympians who live on Mount Olympus, to a multitude of lesser spirits, such as Pan and the nymphs, and demigods, such as Hercules and Achilles who once were mortals.

Gods are just like men, only stronger and cleverer. They like all the same things – food, drink, flowers, dancing and athletic contests – so, to please them, these have to be provided in the form of sacrifices and festivals. Greek temples are erected, not as places where humans come to worship, but as the home of a god or goddess.

The great temple, standing on its stepped platform, consists of three main parts, the entry porch or *pronaos,* the sanctum or *cella* and a chamber at the back, usually the Treasury. All is surrounded by a colonnaded walk between the walls and the rows of Doric pillars.

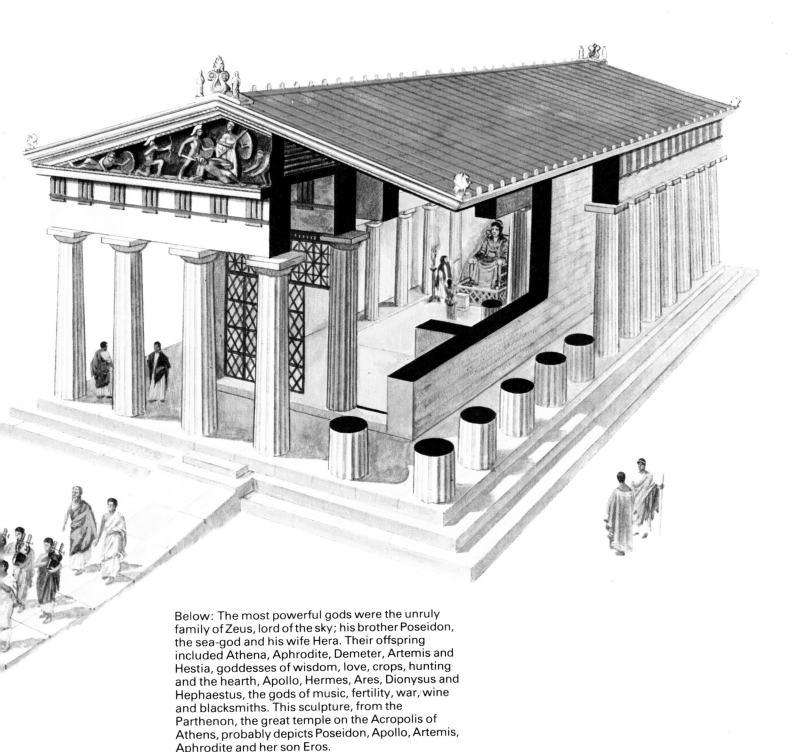

Below: The most powerful gods were the unruly family of Zeus, lord of the sky; his brother Poseidon, the sea-god and his wife Hera. Their offspring included Athena, Aphrodite, Demeter, Artemis and Hestia, goddesses of wisdom, love, crops, hunting and the hearth, Apollo, Hermes, Ares, Dionysus and Hephaestus, the gods of music, fertility, war, wine and blacksmiths. This sculpture, from the Parthenon, the great temple on the Acropolis of Athens, probably depicts Poseidon, Apollo, Artemis, Aphrodite and her son Eros.

At the Theatre

Like most Greek cities, Priene has an open-air theatre, cut out of the side of a hill, so that the tiers of stone seats ascend in a wide semi-circle like a horse shoe. Some theatres, like the famous ones at Athens and Epidaurus, can seat as many as 15,000 persons, for plays are very popular, besides being one of the few public events attended by both men and women.

These plays have developed from thanksgiving festivals hundreds of years ago in Old Greece when people gathered round a circular patch of ground to watch dances in praise of Dionysus, the wine-god. The dancers were known as the *chorus* and their circular dancing-ground was called the *orchestra*.

From these beginnings came the invention of dramatic plays in Athens by three great playwrights, Aeschylus, Sophocles and Euripides who wrote tragedies based on myths and legends and also on historical events like the wars against Troy and the Persians. Later on, Aristophanes and some lesser writers wrote comedies poking fun at well-known people such as politicians and generals.

When a dramatic festival takes place, there are about five days of music and acting, when performances last all day, so the audience bring food and drink with them. They are going to watch three full-length tragedies and a lively farce to finish, so everyone goes home happy.

People used to sit on the grassy hillside to watch but it is now covered by rows of marble benches; down at the front are seats with arms for the priests and important citizens. Everyone has a clear view of the *orchestra* and of the stage beyond, whose lower part, painted to represent doors and pillars, is called the *proscenium*; the chorus comes on to the orchestra from the sides. The stage is backed by a building called the *skene*, in which there are three doors through which the actors make their entrances. The three leading performers, who are always men, use the middle door, while supporting actors go in and out of the other two, but rarely speak.

The Play

By dawn, the theatre is already full, and the play begins with a watchman excitedly shouting that the war against Troy has been won. The chorus of about fifteen men move on to the *orchestra* to perform a solemn dance and to chant their account of the long bitter war. Then the middle door opens and a tall figure appears wearing flowing robes and a huge mask. This is the Queen and presently the King himself arrives, riding in a chariot on his triumphant return from Troy; he too is wearing a face-mask and speaking in verse, for all the dialogue has to be in the form of poetry. He goes into the palace from which a great cry is heard, for he has been murdered, but we don't actually witness the crime, because that is not allowed. Instead, the King's body is wheeled on to the stage, lying on a trolley. So the play goes on and we learn

through long speeches and the appearance of the *chorus* how the murder is avenged and the Queen punished for her treachery. It takes several hours for the grim tragedy to be acted.

If we look closely, we see that the actors appear to be tall because they are wearing shoes with very thick soles and high heels and their robes are padded to increase their girth. The face-masks have a laughing expression for comedy and a mournful one for tragedy and there are other specific masks which always represent, say, an old man, a slave, a flatterer or a hero. The masks act like megaphones and so help the actors' voices to reach people in the most distant seats, but their principal function is to enable the audience, seated in bright sunlight, to recognize each character in the play.

Chapter Six

Loyang, Capital of Han China

This is the city of Loyang in northern China. It lies between the Mang mountains to the north and the Lo river, from which it takes it name. Since AD 25, it has been the capital of the Han empire, replacing the older capital Ch'ang-an which was sacked during a rebellion.

Loyang faces south towards the river and is protected by a wide moat and a thick wall strengthened by towers and bastions. The city, rectangular in shape, measures about two kilometres by three kilometres and is divided into wards by streets running north-south and east-west. Travellers arriving at the capital from all parts of the empire have to pass through one of the massive gates manned by sentinels in the watch-towers above.

The richest and most important part of Loyang is in the north, where the Emperor's palace, set amid gardens and ornamental lakes, is surrounded by a high painted wall. In this

'I have now built this great city here in Lo, considering that there is no central place in which to receive my guests and also that you, ye numerous officers, might here perform the part of ministers to us.'
The Duke of Chou.

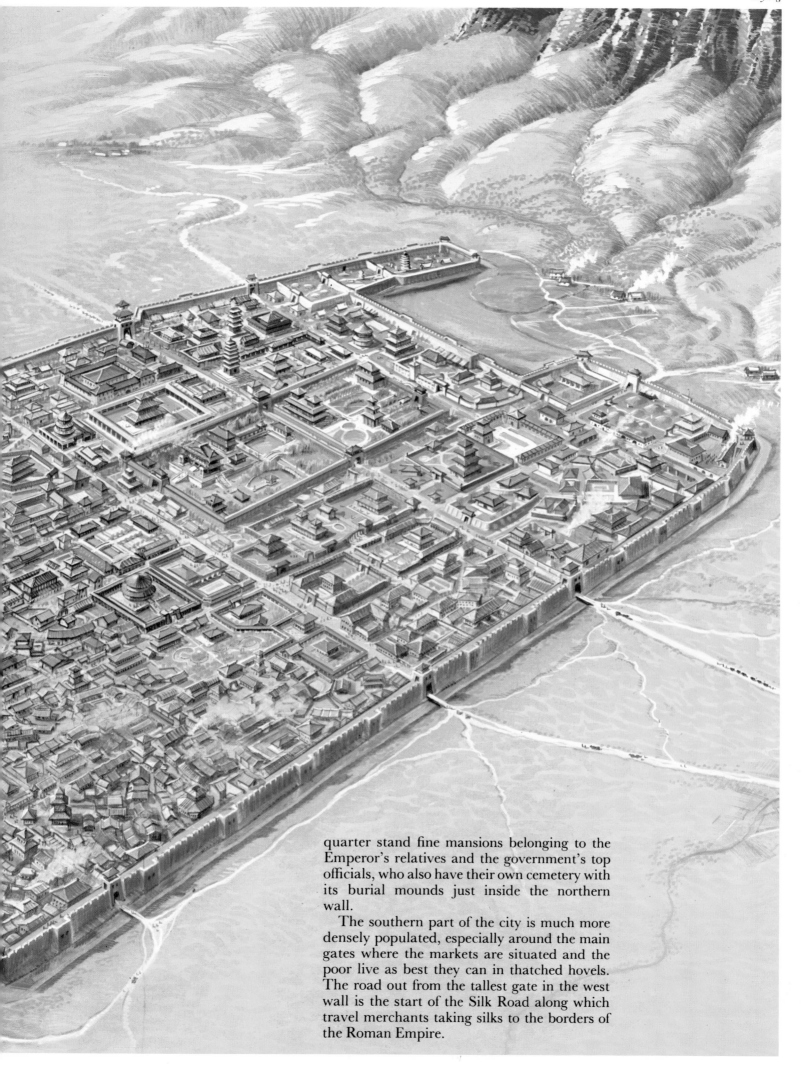

quarter stand fine mansions belonging to the Emperor's relatives and the government's top officials, who also have their own cemetery with its burial mounds just inside the northern wall.

The southern part of the city is much more densely populated, especially around the main gates where the markets are situated and the poor live as best they can in thatched hovels. The road out from the tallest gate in the west wall is the start of the Silk Road along which travel merchants taking silks to the borders of the Roman Empire.

The Market Place

The mass of Han people live in the country and work on the land, but there are also a great many who toil in iron and salt mines, make cloth from silk and hemp, pots, pans, bowls, and lacquered boxes and produce all kinds of metal, wooden and bamboo goods for everyday use. So, although merchants are generally despised, compared with, say, scholars and farmers, they do an essential job in Loyang's markets, catering for the needs of the large population.

Markets are situated near the main gates through which produce arrives daily in wagons and on the backs of pack-animals and porters, to be set out on stalls or simply on the ground where a peasant squats beside the basket of melons or eggs he has brought in from the country. Officials move through the market, collecting taxes in grain or cash from the traders, keeping a sharp watch to see that there is no cheating and turning away vagabonds and beggars who are all too numerous in Chinese towns.

The markets are walled and soon after dawn a drum is beaten to announce that the gates are open to the public who come crowding in to buy meat, poultry, game, dried fish, pickles, fruit and vegetables. Some are looking for leather or sheepskins, mats, curtains or a painted screen; others have come to buy livestock, for there are horses, cattle, sheep and pigs on sale; a farmer may want a pair of new wheels for his ox-cart, while a rich official looks critically at one of the light two-wheeled carriages. In one corner stands a pathetic group of men and women and children waiting to be sold as slaves; some may be prisoners-of-war, while others are relatives of convicted criminals whose goods and chattels have been confiscated. In times of famine and flood disaster, peasants are known to sell their own children into slavery.

The market is the place to go to find the public scribe who writes letters for uneducated people, to listen to a story-teller or to watch the antics of wandering acrobats and jugglers. It is also the place where public announcements are made and, occasionally, where traitors and disgraced ministers are executed by beheading or hanging.

Business in the market may be done by barter or with measures of grain, but, by Han times, a standard coin has come into use – the five-*shu* piece. It is a rectangular copper coin weighing five-*shu* (about three grams) with a hole in the middle so that large numbers can be strung together.

As the day wears on, people can refresh themselves at the cooked-meat stall or with sweet cakes and a cup of soup from the travelling soup-seller, a popular character with his great pot slung from a pole and his fund of local news and gossip. At dusk, the drum booms out its message and the gates are closed for the night.

'It was the struggles of peasants, the peasant uprisings and peasant wars that constituted the real motive force of historical development in Chinese feudal society.'
Chairman Mao, 1939.

Notice the breast-strap harness on the horse-drawn chariot. It is in common use on all vehicles (centuries ahead of anywhere else in the world).

By the wall stand two officials who supervise the trading and collect the trading taxes from the stall-holders. Notice the barber and the Buddhist teacher telling people about a new religion from India.

A Rich Man's House

This house in the northern part of the city belongs to an important official at the Imperial Court and is built in the manner which is common to all kinds of houses (except the hovels of the poor) in Ancient China. It is a luxurious version of a farmhouse, with its entrance gate in the south wall (the direction of holiness) and its various buildings arranged round a courtyard. The whole complex is surrounded by a high wall for security and privacy.

In this house, there is a double courtyard, so that visitors come through the main gate into the outer court where they can leave their smart carriages; then they walk through a doorway into the inner courtyard to mingle with the other guests. Ahead is a handsome building, with two guards stationed at its entrance – an indication of the owner's high rank – and there in the long room upstairs a banquet is taking place. The guests sit on the floor on fur rugs, mats and large colourful cushions. The room is richly decorated with silk hangings, painted screens and large bronze urns full of dried flowers.

To the left of the inner courtyard is a long building containing bedrooms and two private sitting-rooms, a large one for the master and a smaller one for his wife. Adjoining the big house is a smaller one, built in the same way round a courtyard, with an array of many roofed buildings, one with an upper balcony and others with shuttered windows and plaster walls decorated with geometric patterns. The garden is filled with pines, willows and ornamental trees.

Returning to our high official's house, we notice the watchtower rising above the eastern wall from which the household guards keep a constant look-out, because, although Loyang has a police force, the city is plagued from time to time by gangs of youths and lawless ruffians who have made their way to the capital from distant provinces.

Bear's paw and dog-cutlets

The kitchen is situated to the left of the watchtower, well away from the rest of the house so that cooking smells do not offend the aristocrats. Servants have to carry the dishes across the yard, in which there is a pig-sty, and through the courtyard to the banquet.

The guests are regaled with a great many dishes, beginning with a *keng* or stew of beef, mutton or pork and followed by exotic dishes, such as dog-cutlets, bear's paw and panther's breast. They also enjoy fish, kid, quails, bamboo shoots, lotus roots and oranges. Wine, made from grain, is drunk from silver cups.

While they are eating, the diners are entertained by the family's resident musicians who play a variety of instruments such as the traditional bells, drums and flutes, though the lute and the three-stringed zither are now considered to be more fashionable.

The walls surrounding the house are not made of bricks, but of rammed earth, with a tiled roof. The buildings are simple rectangular structures whose roofs are supported by rows of pillars standing on stone bases; the spaces between the pillars are filled with earth plastered over and painted with attractive designs. House

Poor families live in draughty one-room hovels like this one, to which a stable and lean-to shed have been added. It has a thatched roof, a dirt floor and no furniture.

beams and pillars are usually painted in bright colours or given a coating of lacquer, a varnish made from resin, which is coloured, usually red or black, and polished until it shines like glass. Roofs are nearly always covered with semicircular pottery tiles and decorated at the ends and corners with fabulous beasts. Wood and earth are the usual building materials, for stone is only used for an occasional staircase, balustrade or pavement.

Rich people dress in embroidered silk robes, worn with a belt or wide sash. The colours and embroidery patterns are controlled according to a person's rank. Furs and padded clothes are becoming popular in winter, as well as leather trousers and leather belts with jewelled hooks, introduced by the northern nomads. Both men and women pile up their hair into a top-knot which they secure with elaborate hairpins. The Chinese are particularly proud of their shoes which distinguish them from barefooted barbarians. Peasants wear straw sandals but the rich have fine slippers made of damask and brocade.

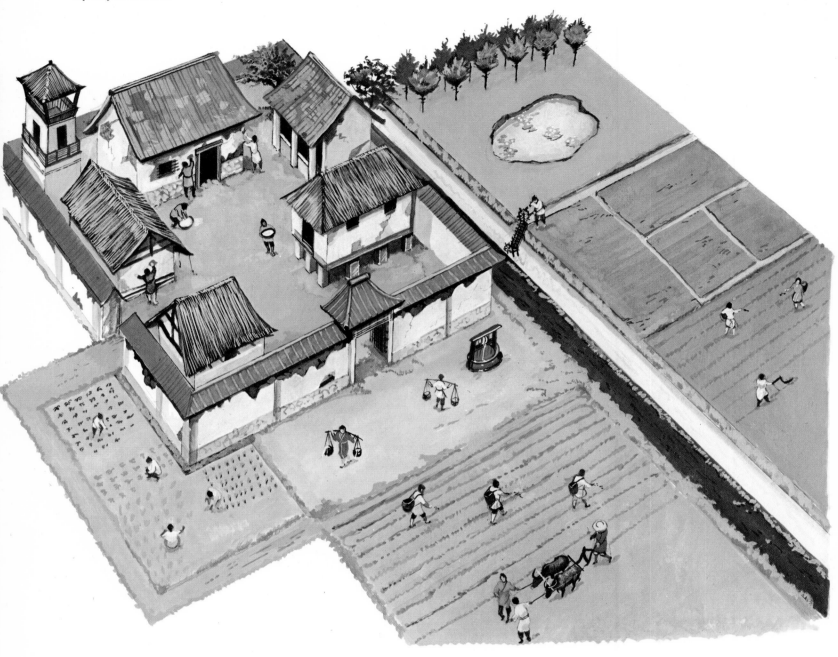

A springtime scene on a farm. It is time for ploughing and sowing. To irrigate the land water is raised from the well in buckets and carried on a pole. A more advanced method is the irrigation machine (which you can see in the picture). The machine consists of a chain of scoops operated by pedals. As they turn, the scoops lift water from the river to the irrigation canals along the fields. Spring is also the time when houses are re-plastered and painted.

The Farmer's Year

The Emperor, the great lords and the host of officials who govern the land all realise that China's prosperity depends on peasants working the land from homesteads like the one in this picture above.

With its protective wall, watchtower and collection of buildings grouped round a yard, this is very much the traditional farmhouse – home of the family who cultivate the surrounding fields of yellow *loess* soil. In the past, a peasant seldom owned his land, but worked on the manor of some powerful lord; however, the Han emperors have given land to the peasants so that many are independent. A small family owning only one or two fields, will combine with several other households to work their land together.

Springtime
This is a springtime scene, the season for ploughing, sowing and planting out, as well as for repairing farm buildings after the winter

storms. Workers irrigate the land with water from the well or use a machine which lifts water from the canal by means of scoops attached to a circular chain. This family owns a pair of oxen; poorer peasants have to harness themselves to the plough.

Taxes
The food for Loyang is produced by peasant farmers who live in riverside villages or homesteads outside the town and who give a proportion of their harvest to the city in the form of a tax. This is a typical homestead where the houses in the villages are two-storeyed and have both tiled and thatched roofs. (We know this from earthenware models that have been found in tombs.)

Threshing and milling are made easier by the use of 'machines'. The corn is threshed using a treadle. The 'pestle' hammer drops down when the foot is raised and so pounds the grain. The grain may be milled with a rotary hand mill. This consists of two interlocking furrowed stones. Grain is poured in through a hole in the top and ground between the rotating stones.

Living off the Land

The farmer's one aim in life is to produce enough to feed and clothe his family and to pay the taxes which will surely be demanded of him. In the north, he mostly grows millet (a grass cereal), wheat and hemp, while, in southern China, the main crop is rice; a good deal of barley is grown in the north-west. Around Loyang, the peasants live mainly on wheat and millet cakes, along with beans, leeks, turnips and cabbages; they use ginger and garlic for flavouring and are fond of peaches, melons and plums. If a family is moderately well-off, a bit of pork, chicken or beef may be added to this diet.

Silk and Hemp

Sheep are kept for mutton and for their warm fleeces, but the Han Chinese do not make woollen cloth, since most people's clothes are made from hemp. Hemp is a tall plant the stems of which are soaked and then dried in the sun to produce a brown fibre which is made into a hardwearing fabric. Rich people prefer silk which comes from caterpillars. These feed on mulberry leaves, so many farmers grow mulberry trees and also lac trees, a species of oak, from which lacquer is made.

Every year, when the harvest is over, men between the ages of 23 and 56 are called up to serve in the state labour corps, building roads and canals or working in the iron and salt mines. Able-bodied men may also have to do two year's service in the Army as frontier guards on the Great Wall or in some campaign to extend the empire.

Above: Autumn on the farm: the ripe grain is harvested and threshed by men using treadles to pound the ears. Some of the grain is ground into flour in a rotary hand-mill and the rest will be stored in the granary, raised up to keep out damp and rats. The women are washing and making clothes.

Below: Winter is the time for mending farm implements and putting by stores of food and fuel. Some of the men are taken away for forced labour and the watchman keeps a lookout for robbers who infest the countryside. In the distance, the gated walls of Loyang are lit by the setting sun.

An hodometer or machine for measuring distance. By means of cogs, one figure strikes the drum after one *li* (500 metres) has been travelled. The other figure sounds the drum after ten *li*. Han scientists also studied the stars and predicted eclipses; they also made an accurate calendar and the first sun dial to measure time.

The first seismograph for recording earthquakes which occur frequently in China. It was invented by Chang Heng (AD 78-139). An earthquake tremor causes the vertical pole to tilt against a trigger which shoots a ball out of the dragon's mouth to the toad below, thus showing the direction of the earthquake.

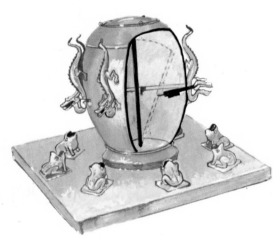

Art and Industry

Not only did the Han dynasty create an efficient government, but it also achieved great things in art, science and industry. Literature flourished, a national library was established and scholars produced history books and one of the world's first dictionaries. Sculptors made many splendid horses and other figures in bronze, jade and terracotta; painting on silk became a fine delicate art and glazed pottery dates from this time.

Han scientists studied the stars, observed sunspots and predicted eclipses; they also made an accurate calendar and the first sun-dial to measure time and the first seismograph for recording earthquakes.

In industry, the government controlled ironmaking. Thanks to the invention of a large piston-bellows, blast furnaces were able to produce cast iron to make all kinds of tools and implements. With iron drills, borings could be made deep into the earth to bring brine (saltwater) to the surface, where it was conveyed in bamboo pipes to pans which were heated until the water evaporated, leaving salt crystals.

Another marvellous achievement was papermanufacture, which you can see going on in the picture below: hemp is soaked and trodden in the river, while potash is being produced in the fire and made into a solution which is mixed with the hemp paste, steamed, pounded, stirred and finally set in frames to dry in the sun.

The tomb of Prince Liu Sheng was discovered in 1968 by soldiers of the People's Liberation Army. Tou Wan, his wife, was buried in a similar tomb hollowed out of the solid rock.

Left: Paper-making – one of the many technical achievements of the Han dynasty. The picture shows different stages in the process: 1. Cutting hemp. 2. Mixing hemp with water. 3. Treading the hemp. 4. Making potash from wood. 5. Making a solution from the potash. 6. Straining the mixture. 7. Mixing ash and hemp paste and steaming it. 8 and 9. Pulping the mixture. 10. Stirring mixture in a bath of clean water. 11. Dipping and removing frames from the mixture. 12. Drying the frames in the sun.

Government

In Han China, the Emperor, 'the son of Heaven', is the leader of his people and the source of all power and authority. From his palace at Loyang, he directs the government by issuing imperial decrees which have to be carried out by state officials throughout the length and breadth of the land. Closest to him are two very senior statesmen, the Prime Minister and the Head of the Civil Service, who confer with the ministers responsible for such important matters as agriculture, taxes, crime, major works, the army, the Court and foreign affairs.

The empire itself is divided into 83 *commanderies* or provinces, each under a Grand Administrator, and 20 kingdoms ruled by the Emperor's own kinsmen. These large areas are divided into *prefectures* and each prefecture is subdivided into districts and each district into wards. Thus, the Emperor's authority reaches out from the capital to the remotest village where local officials collect taxes, try to maintain law and order, keep the roads and canals in order, and direct men to serve in the army and the labour gangs.

Burial Customs and Religion

This picture shows the tomb of Prince Liu Sheng, son of a Han emperor. Discovered in 1968, the body is clad in a suit made of 2498 pieces of jade secured by gold wire. In the tomb are jade objects, bronze vessels and lamps inlaid with gold and silver. In other chambers are models of houses, animals and servants, as well as food, drink and even the Prince's chariot.

Respect for parents and ancestors is immensely important, so the dead are given elaborate funerals and even the poor bury their dead with as much ceremony as possible. The Chinese have always believed in a great number of nature gods and spirits who have to be given respect and sacrifices. They also revere Confucius, a sage who taught the importance of respect for ancestors and parents, of rulers setting a good example and of education and good conduct. Confucianism is a way of life, not a religion. In Han times, Buddhism reached China from India and soon became the country's major religion. The Buddha taught gentleness and loving kindness, rebirth after death and the hope of reaching, through correct living, *nirvana* or everlasting paradise.

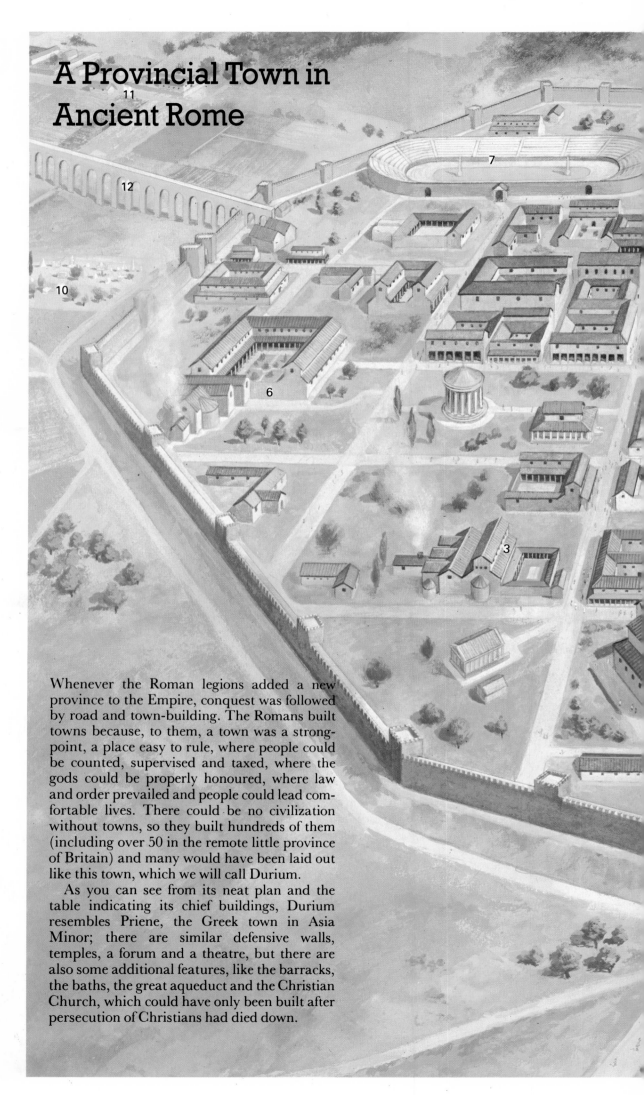

Chapter Seven

A Provincial Town in Ancient Rome

Whenever the Roman legions added a new province to the Empire, conquest was followed by road and town-building. The Romans built towns because, to them, a town was a strong-point, a place easy to rule, where people could be counted, supervised and taxed, where the gods could be properly honoured, where law and order prevailed and people could lead comfortable lives. There could be no civilization without towns, so they built hundreds of them (including over 50 in the remote little province of Britain) and many would have been laid out like this town, which we will call Durium.

As you can see from its neat plan and the table indicating its chief buildings, Durium resembles Priene, the Greek town in Asia Minor; there are similar defensive walls, temples, a forum and a theatre, but there are also some additional features, like the barracks, the baths, the great aqueduct and the Christian Church, which could have only been built after persecution of Christians had died down.

'Rome; everything is found here. All the skills which exist or have existed, anything that can be made or grown. If something can't be found here, then it simply doesn't exist.'
Aelius Aristides,
2nd Century BC.

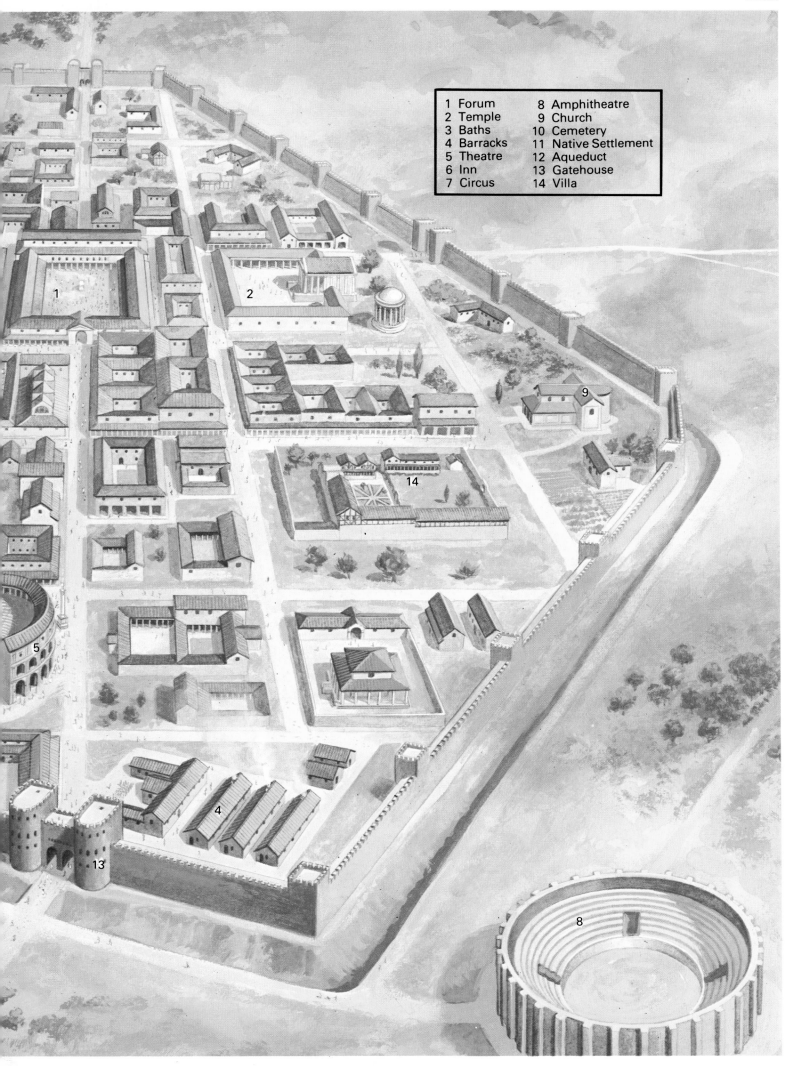

1	Forum	8	Amphitheatre
2	Temple	9	Church
3	Baths	10	Cemetery
4	Barracks	11	Native Settlement
5	Theatre	12	Aqueduct
6	Inn	13	Gatehouse
7	Circus	14	Villa

The Forum

From the town's massive entrance gate, a broad paved road runs dead straight to the *forum*, the open space with its surrounding buildings that corresponds to the Greek *agora* or market-place.

We enter the forum through an imposing archway to find that the open space in the centre is surrounded by a colonnade which is roofed, so that people can walk about or pause to talk to one another in any kind of weather.

To left and right of the entrance archway and within the colonnade are all kinds of shops selling jewellery, textiles, leather goods and household utensils; there are also offices for lawyers, corn-merchants, furriers, inspectors of weights and measures and other officials, and, as you can see in the foreground, a tastefully decorated exchange or bank where business deals are concluded. People can get a bite to eat at one of the cook-shops in the arcade and there are several wine-bars serving hot and cold drinks.

In the open air in the forum itself, country people have set up their stalls to sell produce to trusted slaves who come here to do the daily shopping for their masters' households. No wheeled traffic is permitted in the forum, so people can walk about at their leisure, join in discussions or arguments, exchange news and the latest gossip and stop to listen to a candidate making a speech from the rostrum in which he invites his listeners to vote for him at the coming council elections. The forum is usually adorned with several statues of Roman emperors and notable citizens; there is also a shrine, a drinking fountain and a public lavatory with marble seats!

On the far side, beyond the entrance, stands the *basilica*, the finest building in the whole town, with its rows of magnificent columns supporting an upper floor with windows and the timber and tiled roof. Here, you can see the semi-circular apse where a magistrate is seated on a raised dais, in front of an altar, for the *basilica* is the law court, where cases are heard and judgements are given. The walls are richly decorated with coloured plaster and marble; statues are placed in niches and the floor is paved with mosaic designs. Interested spectators stand about in the nave or in the galleries at first-floor levels to listen to the proceedings, while lawyers meet their clients there and important men try to avoid the idlers and ne'er-do-wells seeking some favour.

Around the great hall of the basilica are the *curia*, the meeting-place of the town council; the *tabularium*, where official documents and records are kept, and the treasury. So that here, under one roof, are all the premises and officials needed to govern and administer the town. You may come across the word *basilica* as meaning a church; this is because, in later times, many basilicas were adapted and used as Christian churches.

Provincial Towns

Coloniae were Roman towns in the provinces built partly to house retired soldiers and to reward them for their service; moreover, they would form a disciplined group to keep order if need be, organize defence and serve on the council. Towns also provided settlement for the conquered tribespeople who might be forcibly moved from their tribal settlements or, better, persuaded to come and live in the town where they would learn Roman ways and perhaps send their sons to school so that they might eventually become citizens of Rome.

Local government is in the hands of the military commander, the magistrate and the town council. Pompeii, destroyed in AD 79, had a council of 100 elected councillors, two chief magistrates and two senior officers (*aediles*) who looked after public order and organization of the Games.

A new town is planned and laid out by army surveyors and the actual building of the walls, temples, public buildings and houses is carried out by soldiers, assisted by local tribesmen.

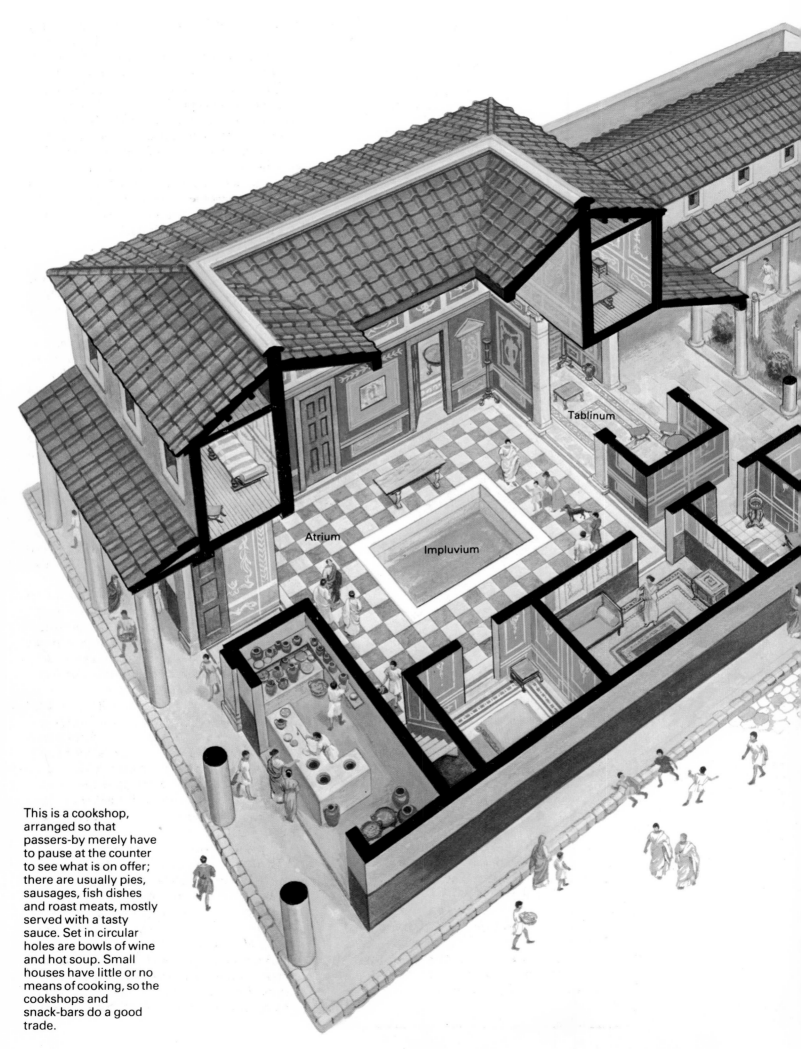

Tablinum

Atrium

Impluvium

This is a cookshop, arranged so that passers-by merely have to pause at the counter to see what is on offer; there are usually pies, sausages, fish dishes and roast meats, mostly served with a tasty sauce. Set in circular holes are bowls of wine and hot soup. Small houses have little or no means of cooking, so the cookshops and snack-bars do a good trade.

A Roman Town House

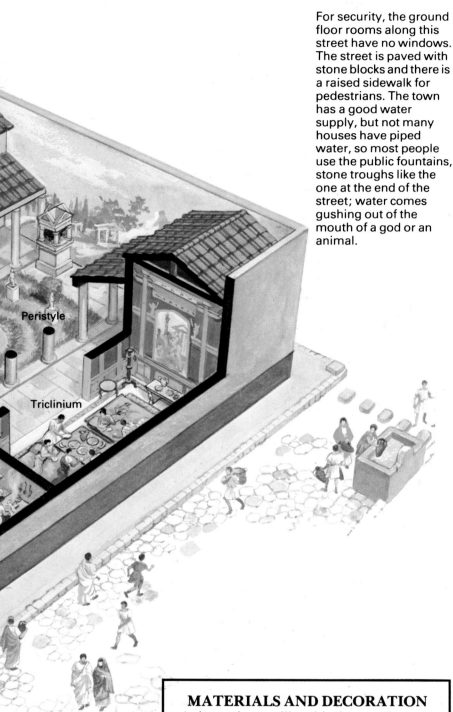

Peristyle

Triclinium

The main rooms have an under-floor heating system. From an outside furnace, hot air is drawn in to circulate round piles supporting the floor, passing up the walls in hollow tiles.

This handsome house, belonging to a wealthy business man, does not look particularly imposing from the street, because its heavy front door is usually shut or guarded by a slave and a fierce dog. This door is flanked by rooms let out as shops, whose rents produce a useful profit.

You enter the house through the *fauces* or passage and come immediately into the *atrium*, a large tiled hall, which has an opening in the roof (the *compluvium*) to let in light, and, at times, rain, which does no harm, because it falls into a pool, *impluvium*, set in the middle of the floor. Gutters and drainpipes also carry rainwater from the roofs to this pool.

Reception rooms

Leading off the atrium are storerooms, the porter's lodge, stairs leading up to the first floor bedrooms and, as you can see on the right, a sitting-room. On the far side of the atrium, beyond the pool, is an elegant room, the *tablinum*, tastefully decorated and furnished. In days gone by, this would have been the dining-room and master-bedroom, but nowadays it is the reception room in which your host greets you and, if it is a fine day, conducts you through to the *peristyle*, a paved colonnade surrounding a charming garden with shrubs, flowers, a fountain and statues of cherubs and nymphs. This is the most private part of the house, where the children play and the family can relax and sometimes take meals in the open air. In the far corner stands the shrine of the household gods, those protective spirits whose images are placed there and given daily offerings of fruit, cakes and incense.

Right of the peristyle is the *triclinium* or dining-room, where the master and his guests, usually a party of nine, dine in luxurious surroundings. Reclined on couches they eat from a low central table, waited upon by a slave, who serves the food and cuts it up so that the diners can eat with the fingers of one hand.

The kitchen, surprisingly small for a large household and placed next to the dining-room for easy service, contains a raised hearth of stone or brick on which the cook heats his pots and pans on iron tripods above charcoal fires. There is usually an oven for cakes and pastry, but bread is bought from the baker's shop down the street. A chimney over the hearth carries away the heat and smoke.

The lavatory is usually next to the kitchen, so that the drains, which run into the public sewer beneath the street, can be close together. Some large houses have their own bathrooms, but most people prefer to go to the public baths where they not only bathe, but meet their friends and generally enjoy themselves.

The bedrooms upstairs have windows looking down on the street; these are fitted with wooden shutters, for glass is rarely used. The slaves' quarters are at the back of the house beyond the peristyle.

MATERIALS AND DECORATION

A large house like this is usually built on low foundation walls of flint and mortar on which a strong timber framework is erected. The spaces between the beams are filled in with rubble and given a coating of plaster, painted on the interior, but left plain outside. The roof is made of red tiles, so heavy that the frame and walls have to be very strong.

Walls of rooms like the *tablinum* and *triclinium* are decorated with *fresco* paintings, that is, painted in water-colours while the plaster is still wet. This is a difficult art, but when the plaster dries, the colours stay bright almost for ever. People like large panels in delicate colours, with patterns, wreaths, urns and imitation marble; scenes with gods and goddesses, birds, animals and landscapes are popular with those who can afford to employ artists from Italy.

The Town's Defences

The Romans established army camps and built forts at strategic points throughout the Empire, linking them and the towns together by splendid roads along which troops could march at speed. They knew, from long experience, that there was always the danger of a local uprising, caused perhaps by the behaviour of some arrogant official, so, in addition to the military camps, they made sure that every town was protected by a massive defensive wall.

When the surveyor responsible for the town layout had decided the position of the wall and its outline had been marked by a plough, soldiers and local labourers would dig a ditch 4 metres deep and 24 metres wide, heaping up the earth on the inner side to provide the 'core' for the wall itself.

The Gatehouse

This is the main gatehouse of Durium, guarding the way into the town and the wooden bridge over the ditch. All wheeled traffic has to pass through the central archway, which can be blocked by lowering a portcullis from an upper chamber; the narrower passages are fitted with heavy wooden doors.

The D-shaped towers of the gatehouse curve outward from the town wall in the form of bastions from which archers and slingers can rake the bridge with cross-fire. Soldiers on the wall-walk can pass through the towers to any point of attack, or up on to the parapet or down into the guard-room, which has a couple of lock-ups behind it for prisoners. Storerooms contain weapons and food and, on top of one tower, you can see a *ballista*, a machine like an outsize cross-bow which fires a heavy javelin.

A Mighty Wall

Across the neck of northern England there still stands a monument to the Roman genius for building defence-works. It is Hadrian's Wall, built to the orders of the Emperor Hadrian, when, on his visit to Britain in AD 122, he decided to fix and defend the Empire's most distant frontier.

The wall, made of stone, with a core of rubble, 2½-metres thick and 6-metres high, runs across wild moors for 117 kilometres. A parapet protected patrols on the wall-walk and there was a ditch beyond the Wall and a communication road running along the inner side. Sentries were housed in 'mile-castles', small forts a Roman mile apart, and at intervals, too, there were turrets with stairs to go up to the wall-walk. The rest of the garrison lived in 19 large forts behind the line of this mighty Wall.

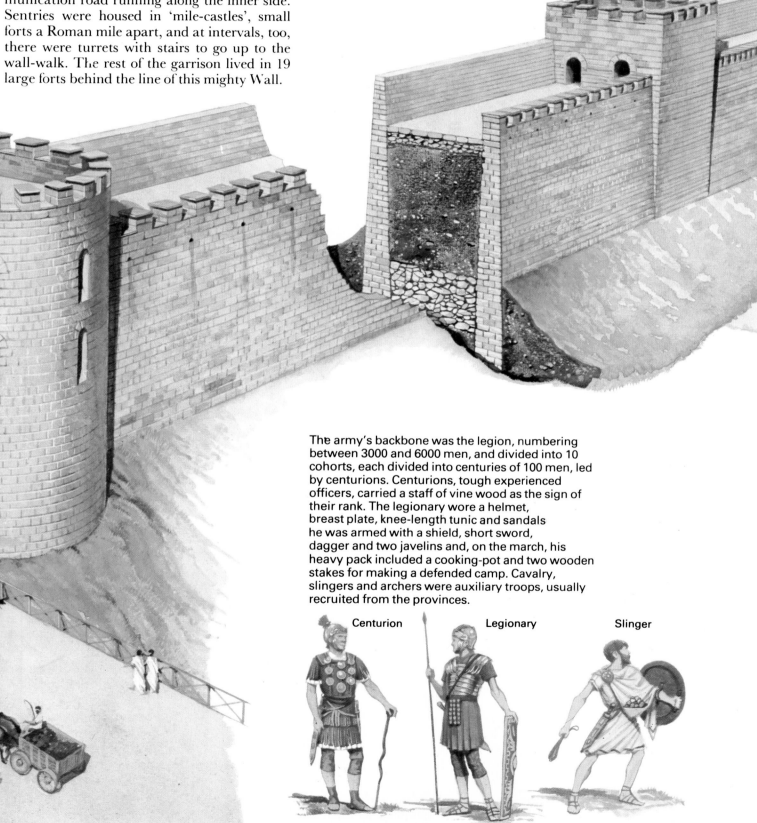

To strengthen Durium's defences, towers are set at intervals along the wall. Notice how the outer wall goes below the surface to foil enemy tunnellers and the inner wall is higher to make it difficult for attackers to fire into the town.

The army's backbone was the legion, numbering between 3000 and 6000 men, and divided into 10 cohorts, each divided into centuries of 100 men, led by centurions. Centurions, tough experienced officers, carried a staff of vine wood as the sign of their rank. The legionary wore a helmet, breast plate, knee-length tunic and sandals he was armed with a shield, short sword, dagger and two javelins and, on the march, his heavy pack included a cooking-pot and two wooden stakes for making a defended camp. Cavalry, slingers and archers were auxiliary troops, usually recruited from the provinces.

Centurion   Legionary   Slinger

Gladiators and Charioteers

As we have seen at the businessman's house in Durium, Romans like to live in comfort, even luxury, but, of course, only the rich can afford elegant dining-rooms and the performances of musicians and dancing-girls in their own homes. The rest of the population, including the poor, whose houses are wretchedly built and practically without furniture, not only find plenty of amusement in the streets, forum, and at the Baths, but in the various entertainments that are put on for their benefit during festivals and public holidays.

There are three main kinds of entertainment, the Theatre, where plays are produced; the Amphitheatre, where people go to see fights to the death between gladiators; and the Circus, which is mainly used for chariot-races. The cost of these shows to the public is very little – indeed many of them are free, because wealthy citizens pay for them, either from a sense of duty or in order to get themselves elected to high office in the town.

However, in Durium, as in most provincial towns, there is not the same enormous idle population as in Rome itself, fed by the State and demanding to be constantly entertained because it has nothing to do. At Durium, things are different, for this is a busy town, devoted to business and industry and not containing mobs of unemployed. Nevertheless, the Theatre, Circus and Amphitheatre are well patronized, since there are many religious and civic holidays, when practically the entire population, including women, children and slaves, turns out to enjoy themselves.

In this theatre both Roman and Greek plays are performed. This play ends with someone being killed; at the last moment the actor's place will be taken by a condemned man who will actually be killed on stage.

At the Games

No other entertainment can compare with the Games at the Amphitheatre and, when a holiday show is announced, everyone dashes along in good time to get the best seat he can. By the time the spectacle starts there is not a seat to be had. Women watch from boxes in the gallery round the top.

The show starts with a parade of the gladiators, who are received with frenzied cheers by the fans; next, the director of the games consecrates the spectacle to the spirits of the dead, for it is blood and death that the people have come to see. A boxing-match follows and perhaps a mock battle between teams armed with blunt weapons, but the crowd is soon yelling for the real thing and on comes the first pair of gladiators, a *retiarius*, armed with a net and a trident, and a *mirmillo*, in helmet, with a shield and short sword. Their's is a desperate contest, savage and skilful, until the mirmillo slips and falls hopelessly entangled in the net. Is he to live or die? The spectators turn down their thumbs, the dagger does its work and slaves drag the body away and rake the bloodstained sand for the next bout. As a change, this may be a fight between gladiators on horseback, armed with lances.

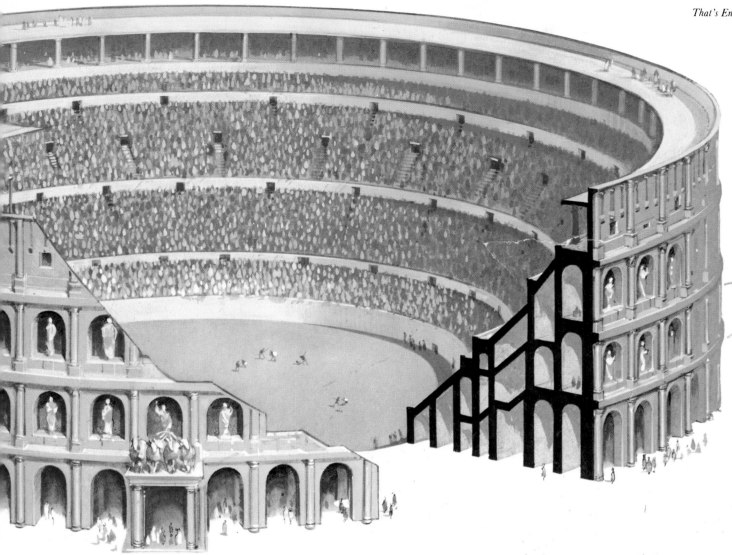

The Gladiators

Gladiators are nearly always slaves, criminals or prisoners-of-war, but success brings such fame and glory that freemen sometimes take up this dangerous career. No matter how many their victories – and some gladiators have won more than 50 contests – nearly all will perish in the arena. Just a few survive and retire to teach novices at a training school or manage one of the troops that tour the provinces – a tame alternative to these brave men.

Another bloodthirsty show is the *venatio*, a sham hunt, when wild animals are let into the arena – lions, panthers, bears, boars and harmless gazelles – to be speared by men behind grilles or made to fight and tear one another to pieces.

On the other side of the town is the Circus, a big oval track, where huge crowds come to watch chariot-racing. This is a most exciting sport in which two-, three- or four-horse chariots tear down the straight and round the sharp bends for seven laps at such tremendous speed that there are many collisions and accidents. But, if he survives, a star charioteer will make a fortune and become even more of a popular hero than the best of the gladiators or charioteers.

At the Theatre

Durium's theatre closely resembles a Greek theatre, except that the Romans have cut the *orchestra* in half, so that it is a semi-circle. This is still used occasionally by actors, but it is mostly a privileged space where important persons sit on comfortable chairs in front of the stage, which is fitted with a curtain lowered into a slot just before a performance begins.

Plays range from Greek tragedies, which appeal to the more cultured townsfolk, to comedies, mimes and downright knock-about farces. These last were originally put on after a tragedy to make sure the audience went home in a happy mood, but nowadays, they are so popular that they have become the main attraction. People roar with laughter at the antics of well-known characters such as Maccus, the greedy-guts who turns banker, Pappus the fool who wants to be a magistrate and Bucco, the hunchback, who tries his hand as a gladiator. The show finishes with comic mimes, dancers, acrobats, jugglers and nude chorus girls.

Unlike the Greeks, Romans allow women to appear on the stage, so there are popular actresses, as well as some famous actors, though their profession is looked on as a rather lowly one.

Above: An amphitheatre like this one seats up to 20,000 spectators; many come into the town from miles around. There are so many entrance arches that the audience can come and go easily. Between the banks of seats and the outer wall two concentric walls form a colonnade on the ground floor and a gallery at the top. A giant awning is fixed in strips over the enclosure to shade the audience from the sun.

Chapter Eight

The Aztecs

Mexico is a land of mountains and volcanoes, deserts and fertile valleys and it was here that the Olmec civilization flourished from 1000 BC until it was destroyed in about AD 700 by barbarians from the north called Chichimecs. More invaders, including the fierce Toltecs, poured into the rich Valley of Mexico, bringing their blood-drinking gods with them and founding small city-states which were constantly at war with one another.

Last of the newcomers, the Aztecs reached the Valley in about AD 1200, a despised semi-barbaric tribe who, finding that all the good farmland was already occupied, took refuge on the marshy islands of Lake Texcoco.

By dredging mud from the bottom of the shallow lake to enlarge the islands, they created the city of temples, palaces, canals and houses shown here and they called it Tenochtitlan, the Place of the Prickly Pear Cactus.

'The people of this land are well made, rather tall than short. They are swarthy as leopards, of good manners and gestures, for the greater part very skilful, robust and tireless. They are very warlike and face death with the greatest resolution,'
Anonymous soldier in Cortes' army.

With over 300,000 inhabitants, Tenochtitlan exceeds any European city of its time in size and magnificence.

Between the city and the snow-capped mountains is a fertile plain dotted with towns and villages. The Aztecs soon conquered them all.

The 15-km dyke prevents salty water from polluting the *chinampas*, 'floating gardens' — islands planted with vegetables which you can see all round the city.

Causeways, wide enough for horsemen to ride three abreast, link the Aztec capital to the mainland. An aqueduct brings fresh water into the city.

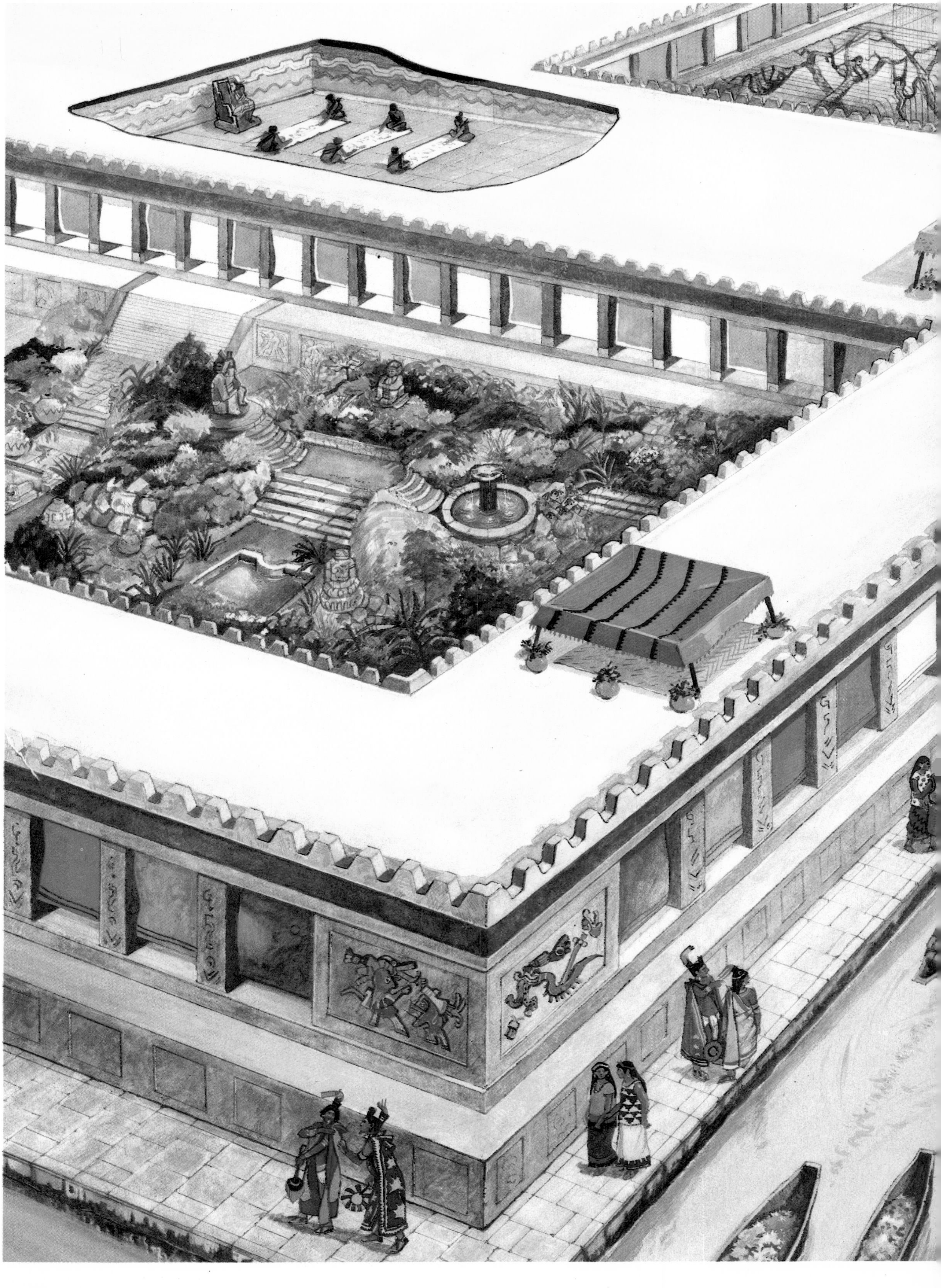

Montezuma's Palace

In this city of canals, which act as highways for hundreds of flat-bottomed canoes transporting goods and produce and which are bordered by pedestrian lanes, the Royal Palace stands in the centre, next to the Temple Precinct. It is so vast that it not only houses the Emperor and his household, but some 3,000 state officials who live and work in scores of rooms and offices. The palace also contains law-courts, the treasury, an arsenal of weapons, a prison and guest-rooms for important visitors; in fact, there are so many halls, courtyards and corridors that men say you can walk all day and never come to an end of it.

One hall, big enough to accommodate 3,000 persons, is faced with polished stone and sculptures of gods, warriors and strange legendary creatures such as you can see here. There is colour everywhere – panels, curtains, roof-awnings and in the robes of the nobles, who, unlike the common people, are allowed to dress in brilliant colours. Some of the rooms are decorated with painted designs, others with gold and silver plaques and there are 100 bedrooms each with a stone bath and running water.

The royal gardens are filled with all kinds of shrubs and flowers, which Aztecs love passionately, and there is a zoo stocked with jaguars, deer, monkeys, snakes and raccoons.

Montezuma

The Emperor, who dwells in such fantastic splendour, is treated like a god, for no-one, not even the nobles and high priests who attend him, may raise their eyes to look him in the face. He eats his meals alone, behind a gilded screen and, on the rare occasions when he leaves the palace, he is carried by eight lords in a litter like a throne, surmounted by a gorgeous canopy, and he wears a jewelled crown topped by green plumes, a feather cloak and robes glittering with jewels. Even his sandals are of pure gold and when he walks, the ground is covered by cloth so that his feet do not touch it.

On the Emperor's death, a council of nobles choose his successor, always from the royal family, who may be one of his many sons or, more likely, his brother.

'The great city . . . has many broad streets, half of each one is of hard earth, and the other half is by water, so that they leave in their canoes or barks. . . . The inhabitants go for a stroll, some in canoes and others along the land, and keep up conversations.'
Anonymous soldier in Cortes' army.

Aztec canoes are hollowed out tree trunks. Here, canoes full of baskets, *papaya* (a large orange fruit), bundles of cloth and flowers are being punted to the market. A man is buying a bunch of flowers to hide the smells of decaying flesh drifting across from the Temple Precinct.

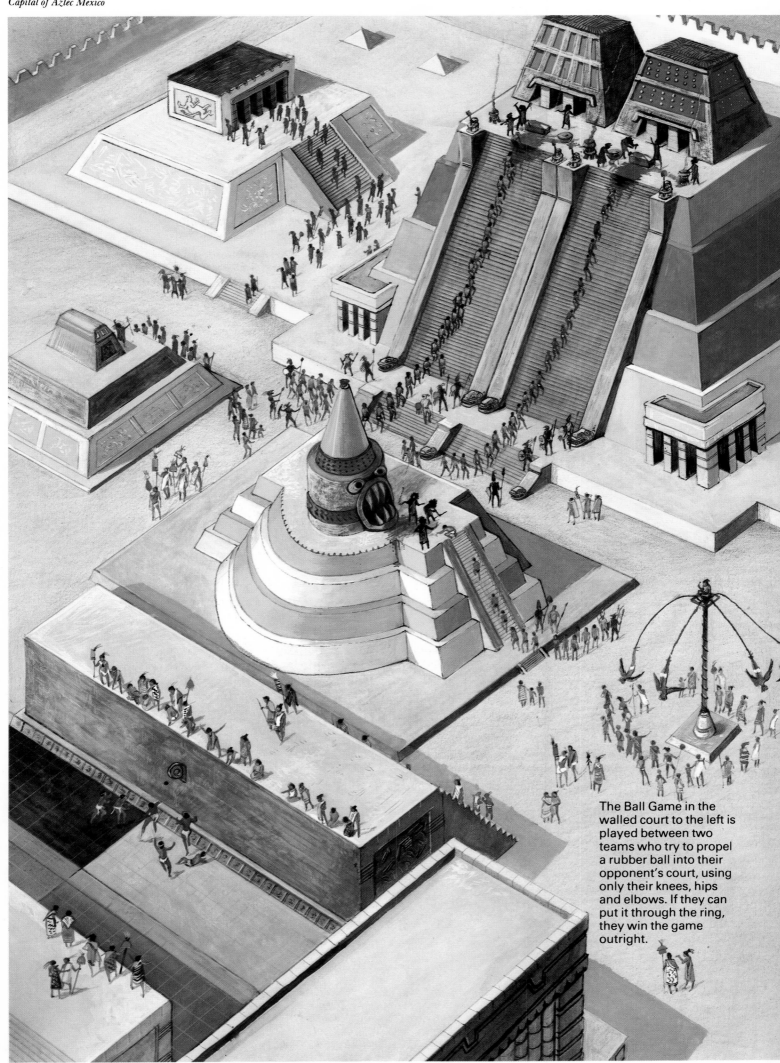

The Ball Game in the walled court to the left is played between two teams who try to propel a rubber ball into their opponent's court, using only their knees, hips and elbows. If they can put it through the ring, they win the game outright.

Priests are everwhere. Dressed in dark robes embroidered with skulls, their long hair matted with blood and their bodies painted black, they go about beating themselves with thorns.

The tall pole in the courtyard has four men dressed as birds, attached by ropes in such a way as to rotate, so they fly like the gods.

Blood for the Gods

In the city centre, where the three causeways meet, is the Temple Precinct, a vast enclosure surrounded by a wall decorated with carved serpents and containing a great pyramid-temple. Its double-staircase leads up to a pair of temples, one belonging to Tlaloc, the Rain God, and the other to Huitzilopochtli or the Left-handed Humming Bird, the Sun God and greedy God of War. Two stone altars stand outside on a terrace.

Down below in the courtyard stands another temple with a door shaped like a devil's mouth which is fed with sacrificed human bodies. This temple is sacred to Quetzalcoatl, the Plumed Serpent, an ancient god who has departed but will return one day bringing disaster to the land.

The Temple Precinct also contains a building filled with thousands of skulls, houses for the priests, a college of novices, several sacrificial altars and the Court of the Sacred Ball Game.

Aztecs believe that the gods cause the sun to rise each morning and to die every night; they bring rain, the drought, illness and death; they are watching all the time and they have to be fed and kept strong, so that the sun may come back to life every day. Otherwise, all light and life will vanish from the earth. Therefore men must give them the most precious thing they possess which is blood from the human heart. Accordingly, the sacrificial victims, mostly prisoners captured in battle, mount the steps leading to the altars; they do not have to be driven, for they have no fear of death, knowing it is an honour to help nourish the gods and become in a sense part of the sun.

Each victim is stretched out upon the altar; a priest plunges a knife into his chest, removes the heart and holds it up to the gods. In the temples, fellow-priests pour bowls of blood over the heads of giant idols, while the victims' heads are placed on the skull racks and their limbs cut into small pieces and distributed to the congregation to eat.

In order to obtain an unceasing supply of victims for the gods, the Aztecs wage continuous war on their neighbours, so every young man is trained to fight and above all to capture prisoners alive. When he has taken four prisoners in battle, he will be rewarded with gifts and slaves. Successful warriors are honoured above all other men and often become judges and governors of conquered provinces.

This Eagle Knight has a helmet shaped like an eagle's head with gaping beak, he wields a battle-axe; other warriors carry shields, lances, slings, bows and wooden swords edged with razor-sharp stones. Jaguar Knights wear ocelot skins. Their faces peer out of the animal's jaws.

The Life of the People

In spite of their fearful religion, Aztecs are quiet, law-abiding people, with a strong sense of duty and respect for their elders. They enjoy pageant-like festivals when there is dancing in the city squares and, at midsummer, they go out into the country to gather flowers to decorate the temples. At harvest-time, when the Emperor gives food and drink to the entire population, there is a whole week of feasting and dancing.

Most people work on the land, growing food to feed their families and all the officials who run the state. Taxes have to be paid in food-stuffs, chiefly maize, but there is a scheme to help widows and orphans.

In the pictures, you can see people living and working on the *chinampas*, the island gardens that produce much of Tenochtitlan's food. Men pile up reeds and vegetation to make artificial islands which are topped up with fertile mud and held together by wooden piles and the roots of willow trees. Once established, the *chinampas* produce abundant crops of vegetables, such as beans, tomatoes, chilli peppers, onions and a great deal of maize, the staple food for everyone. Here and in the mainland fields, all cultivation is done with a broad-bladed digging-stick, because the Aztecs have no ploughs or carts of any kind.

Meat is a luxury reserved for special meals and feast-days, when a turkey will be killed or perhaps one of the little hairless dogs which are kept as pets and fattened for the table. Hunting parties sometimes bring home deer, hares, rabbits and wild pigs from the forests. Rich nobles can afford exotic dishes such as oysters and seafish brought up from the coast, pineapples from the Hot Lands and chocolate drinks flavoured with vanilla.

In the city itself people live together in clans, groups of about twenty families, each with its own temple and school, under a leader who acts as mayor of the district. Some citizens are expert craftsmen, working as stonemasons, goldsmiths, jewellers, carpenters, potters, mosaic-workers and makers of the brilliantly coloured feather cloaks and headdresses that are worn by nobles and warriors. Craftsmen and merchants tend to stick together and to pass on their trade secrets from father to son. Outside the clans are two lower classes, the *mayeques* or landless labourers, and slaves who have been captured in battle or arrested for crime or debt.

Children have a strict upbringing and most boys go to the local clan school, where retired warriors teach history, religion, music, dancing and, above all, good behaviour. There are no lessons in reading and writing, for the whole aim is to toughen the boys and turn them into good citizens. Sons of nobles have an even harsher schooling at the hands of priests who make them go on endurance tests in the mountains, but they also learn writing, mathematics, astrology, law and medicine.

The End of a Civilization

The truly remarkable thing about the civilizations of ancient America is their complete isolation from the rest of the world. All the civilizations of the Old World came into contact at some stage with other peoples, ideas and cultures. The Egyptians, for instance, learnt how to smelt iron from the Hittites; the Indus Valley people traded with the Sumerians; the Chinese, isolated for a long time, gained a major religion from India and commercial goods from the Roman world; the Greeks learned much from Asiatics, the Romans learned from the Greeks and the whole of Europe eventually obtained all kinds of knowledge from the Chinese.

A Hidden Civilization

But none of this was possible for the peoples of Mexico and Peru. Hidden behind the oceans, they had to find out everything for themselves and yet built civilizations that were astonishingly like those of the Old World. They invented similar systems of government, town life, housing, water-supply, agriculture, trade, religion and warfare. The most obvious differences were their lack of large domestic animals, the absence of wheels and vehicles, their ignorance of iron and their failure to devise an effective written language. Nor did they possess, in the year 1519, any firearms.

Quetzalcoatl returns

In 1519, Montezuma II, the Aztec Emperor, had been ruling his empire of many peoples and hundreds of towns for 17 years. His power was immense, and the empire was at its peak, yet disturbing rumours were reaching Tenochtitlan of a strange and terrible people arriving on the islands off the coast. And now some of them had reached the mainland and were advancing towards the capital, under a leader possessing all the attributes of the god Quetzalcoatl, who was due to return to Mexico this very year.

Hernando Cortes

The leader was Hernando Cortes, a Spaniard of iron determination and infinite resource who led his force of 500 adventurers into the heart of the Aztec capital where Montezuma accorded him all the reverence due to a god. Thirsting for gold, Cortes suddenly turned on his host, who was killed in a riot; then, with the aid of local tribes who hated the Aztecs, Cortes laid siege to the lake-city, cut its fresh water supply, and, after a desperate struggle, captured it and massacred all who failed to escape to the mainland. Broken by this disaster and the arrival of the white men's disease, smallpox, the Aztecs abandoned resistance, as their empire fell to pieces and their short-lived civilization came to an end.

Above: Building a *chinampa*. In the background, men are trying to spear a heron, trapping birds in flight with an ingenious net and skimming the water for masses of insect eggs which are eaten as a delicacy. The lake also yields fish, waterfowl, frogs and shrimps for the larder.

Below: Going to market. A *chinampa* family loads the canoe with honey from the hives next to the house and colourful rugs woven at home. Notice the turkeys, the parrot which acts as a watchdog, the household goddess, rolling pin and stone slab and the flat maize cakes cooked fresh for every meal.

Date Chart

(Note: most dates in ancient times are uncertain, so that even experts disagree about many of them; c., from the Latin *circa*, meaning 'about' is placed in front of doubtful dates)

BC

c. 4000	City-states begin to arise in Sumeria.
c. 3500	Temple-building and first cuneiform writing.
c. 3300	Menes unites Upper and Lower Egypt.
c. 3000-2600	Pyramid Age in Egypt: hieroglyphic writing emerges.
c. 2500	Rise of Indus civilization.
c. 2370	Sargon of Akkad ruled in Sumeria.
c. 2200-1500	Legendary Hsia dynasty in China.
c. 2100-2000	Kings of Ur supreme in Mesopotamia.
c. 2100-1750	Middle Kingdom of Egypt.
c. 2000	Minoan civilization in Crete. Hittites found a strong kingdom. Village life in Mexico.
c. 1792-1750	Hammurabi, King of Babylon.
c. 1750-1550	Hyksos (Shepherd Kings) rule Nile Delta.
c. 1750-1027	Shang dynasty in China: Chinese writing founded.
c. 1600-1200	Mycenaean civilization on Greek mainland.
c. 1550-1085	The New Kingdom of Egypt: 18th Dynasty. Pharaohs establish the Empire. Era of temple-building.
c. 1500	Mohenjo-Daro destroyed. Ayrans enter India.
c. 1400	Egyptian Empire at its peak. City of Knossos in Crete destroyed.
c. 1375	Akhetaten built.
c. 1300	Wars between Egypt and Hittites.
c. 1225	Moses leads Israelites out of Egypt.
c. 1200	Greeks capture Troy.
c. 1100	Dorians invade Greece. Rise of the Assyrians.
c. 1027	Chou dynasty overcomes the Shang.
c. 1000-400	Olmec culture in central America.
c. 850	Homer composes the *Iliad* and the *Odyssey*.
c. 813	Carthage founded in N. Africa.
776	First recorded Olympic Games.
753	Legendary foundation of Rome.
721	Chou capital removed to Loyang.
701	Sennacherib makes Nineveh the Assyrian capital.
689	Assyrians destroy Babylon.
670	Medes and Chaldeans overthrow Assyrian Empire.
c. 600	Nebuchadnezzar rebuilds Babylon. Priene founded in Asia Minor.
c. 530	Confucius teaching in China, Buddha in India.
525	Persians conquer Egypt.
499	Persians conquer Ionian colonies in Asia Minor.
490	Greeks defeat Persians at Marathon.
480-221	Period of Warring States in China.
460-429	Athens controlled by Pericles. Parthenon built.
431-404	War between Athens and Sparta.
396	Romans defeat the Etruscans.
338	Philip of Macedon, master of Greece.
334-323	Alexander the Great overthrows the Persian Empire.
275-232	Rule of Asoka in India.
264-202	Punic Wars: Rome overcomes Carthage.
c. 256-206	Ch'in Dynasty in China: despotic rule of Huang-Ti; Great Wall built.
206	Han dynasty founded.
146	Greece becomes a Roman province.
141-87	Peak of Han Empire under Wu Ti.
58-49	Julius Caesar's campaigns in Gaul.
44	Julius Caesar murdered.
27 BC-AD 14	Augustus Caesar rules the Roman Empire.
AD 25	Loyang the capital of the Han Empire.
c. 60	Buddhism enters China.
98-117	Trajan expands the Roman Empire.
117-138	Emperor Hadrian.
220	Han dynasty overthrown.
c. 300-900	Maya civilization in Central America.
330	Constantine makes Byzantium the capital of the Roman Empire.
410	Rome sacked by the Goths.
476	Last Roman Emperor deposed.
c. 700	Chichimecs destroy Teotihuacan in Mexico.
c. 975	Toltecs rule in Central America.
c. 1200	Aztecs settle in Valley of Mexico.
1325	Tenochtitlan built.
c. 1400-1500	Inca Empire at its peak in S. America.
1519-21	Cortes defeats the Aztecs and destroys Tenochtitlan.

Index

THE AZTECS
OF MEXICO
AD 1500

The Mayas
AD 200-600

The Incas
1400-1532

The Norsemen
1500-500 BC

ANCIENT ROM
IN AD 117

The Nok
500 BC-AD 200